# Foreword

'Betting The Timeform Way' concentrates on providing helpful information for those who take betting on horses seriously, or aspire to do so.

The book is not written for those who believe that base metal can be turned into gold. Those supreme optimists who go into a betting shop looking for a big pay-day for a small outlay will gain no comfort from the pages that follow. The many widely-advertised cumulative bets so popular with Mr and Mrs Average Punter contribute more to bookmakers' sunshine cruises than any other form of betting. This way of betting is a mug's game.

The vast majority of punters lose because they don't understand what is involved. But there are shrewd backers who *do* make a profit out of betting on horses. Many of them use publications such as the Timeform Weekly Black Books, the Timeform Perspective form-book and the daily Timeform Race Cards, in which nearly all the hard groundwork requisite to success in racing is already done for them.

But finding winners is only half the battle. A *probable winner* and a *betting opportunity* aren't one and the same. No-one makes a profit in the long run unless he or she has a grasp of the mathematics of betting and fully understands odds and 'value'.

We hope this book will help the reader to a clearer understanding of what is involved and put him or her on the road to becoming a consistently successful punter.

December 1993

# Contents

## The Mathematics

## In Practice

© Portway Press Limited 1993

Betting The Timeform Way is printed and published
by Portway Press Limited, Halifax, West Yorkshire HX1 1XE.
It is supplied to the purchaser for his personal use and on the understanding that its contents
are not disclosed. Every care is taken in the compilation of Betting The Timeform Way but no
responsibility is accepted by the publishers for errors or omissions or their consequences.

ISBN 0 900599 67 7

# Betting The Timeform Way:

## The Mathematics

There are two types of bettor, the one who wagers on the outcome of an event (the backer) and the one who stands the wager (the layer or bookmaker). Their roles are well defined. And dissimilar. So one would think. But are they? Take the case where just one bet is struck. As an instance, let us suppose the backer has a bet on Cambridge at even money to win the Boat Race, dead-heat no bet. Now backer and layer are firmly on the same side of the fence. The backer is on Cambridge at even money and the layer is on Oxford at the same price. An even bet? Well, not exactly. As we all know, it is unusual for both contestants, be they in the Boat Race, a boxing match, a football game, or whatever, to be matched so evenly that their chances are widely considered to be one and the same. Almost invariably the form of one will be such as to suggest it has a better than even chance (odds on) of winning whilst the other will be considered to have a worse than even chance (odds against). The bookmaker bases his odds on his evaluation of the form factor, and 'adjusts' those odds—shortens them, if you prefer the word—to take account of the profit he hopes to make. This 'profit' element is present in all transactions between backer and bookmaker and is known by the bookmaker as his theoretical profit margin. With emphasis on the word theoretical. The effect of the bookmaker's profit margin is seen most clearly in those cases where the backer chooses between two, as in our Boat Race example, for instance. For the backer here to be able to bet on Cambridge at even money, means that the bookmaker will have Oxford at 4/6. Or thereabouts. The bookmaker's profit margin—more popularly known as his percentage—has placed our Cambridge backer in the dubious position where he finds himself either 'laying' the bookmaker even money about an odds-on chance, or 'accepting' even money from the bookmaker about an odds-against chance. Either way it doesn't make sense. Not when all our backer has to do in such circumstances is to seek out, if he can, an acquaintance who fancies the other 'side'—in this case Oxford—and come to some arrangement. For our

Cambridge backer even 6/5 would be worth the effort. Maybe it doesn't seem to matter all that much whether the backer gets 1/1 or 6/5 for his money so long as his bet wins. But it does. The backer cannot always be on the winner, and the importance of his getting the best possible price when his bet does win needs to be stressed. Few professionals make 10% on turnover in the long run. The difference between 1/1 and 6/5 is 20% of the outlay and getting always the better or always the worse of the two prices may mean the difference in the long run between making a slight profit and making a slight loss. This is why professional backers, calmly standing aside when 1/1 is on offer, may very well pounce like a cat in their eagerness to get 'on' when the price is lengthened even as little as to 6/5. Successful backing is all about the search for value. Of getting the best of the odds.

## Odds And Chances

Most racegoers know that if there are four runners with equal chances in a race, it is 3/1 against each of them. One pound on each runner at 3/1 leaves the backer all square whatever the result. 3/1 is therefore the correct price, which favours neither layer nor backer. As there are four runners, each has a quarter chance of winning. To put it mathematically, the chance (or probability) of each runner individually is ¼. First of all, observe that the chances of the four runners together adds up to 1. This is not an accident; it follows from the definition of chance. No matter how many runners there are in a race, and no matter whether they have equal chances or not, the sum total of the true chances of the runners added together is always 1.

Secondly, note that odds of 3/1 are equivalent to a chance of ¼. They are merely two ways of putting the same thing. Sometimes it is more convenient to speak in terms of odds—when making a bet, for example—but at other times the use of chances instead is essential. To transform odds to chances is straightforward for anyone with a mathematical inclination. Add up both sides of the odds and place the result underneath the right-hand side of the odds. Thus, if the horse is 3/1, three and one are four and its chance is therefore ¼; if the horse is 6/4, six and four are ten and its chance is ⁴⁄₁₀; if it is 6/4 on, i.e. 4/6, its chance is ⁶⁄₁₀. These fractional chances should be

4

| | Table of Odds and Chances | | |
|---|---|---|---|

| Odds | Odds on chance | Odds against chance |
|---|---|---|
| Evens | .500 | .500 |
| 21/20 | .512 | .488 |
| 11/10 | .524 | .476 |
| 6/5 | .545 | .455 |
| 5/4 | .556 | .444 |
| 11/8 | .579 | .421 |
| 6/4 | .600 | .400 |
| 13/8 | .619 | .381 |
| 7/4 | .636 | .364 |
| 15/8 | .652 | .348 |
| 2/1 | .667 | .333 |
| 85/40 | .680 | .320 |
| 9/4 | .692 | .308 |
| 5/2 | .714 | .286 |
| 11/4 | .733 | .267 |
| 3/1 | .750 | .250 |
| 100/30 | .769 | .231 |
| 7/2 | .778 | .222 |
| 4/1 | .800 | .200 |
| 9/2 | .818 | .182 |
| 5/1 | .833 | .167 |
| 11/2 | .846 | .154 |
| 6/1 | .857 | .143 |
| 13/2 | .867 | .133 |
| 7/1 | .875 | .125 |
| 15/2 | .883 | .117 |
| 8/1 | .889 | .111 |
| 17/2 | .895 | .105 |
| 9/1 | .900 | .100 |
| 10/1 | .909 | .091 |
| 11/1 | .917 | .083 |
| 12/1 | .923 | .077 |
| 13/1 | .929 | .071 |
| 14/1 | .933 | .067 |
| 15/1 | .938 | .062 |
| 16/1 | .941 | .059 |
| 18/1 | .947 | .053 |
| 20/1 | .952 | .048 |
| 22/1 | .957 | .043 |
| 25/1 | .962 | .038 |
| 28/1 | .966 | .034 |
| 33/1 | .970 | .030 |
| 40/1 | .976 | .024 |
| 50/1 | .980 | .020 |
| 66/1 | .985 | .015 |
| 100/1 | .990 | .010 |

transformed into decimals by dividing the top of the fraction by the bottom: thus, ¼ becomes .250, ⅛ becomes .125, and so on. A full table of odds and chances is given above. The reader will find it a very valuable table, and he should practise using it, in ways that follow, as often as possible, so as eventually to have the principal odds and equivalent chances off by heart.

# What The Backer Is Up Against

The table enables us to find out the *theoretical* margin to which the bookmaker works. As an example, consider the Coalite St Leger Stakes, run at Doncaster on September 12th, 1992, race 3156 in *Timeform Perspective*.

| Horses | Odds | Chances |
|---|---|---|
| User Friendly | 7/4 | .364 |
| Bonny Scot | 5/2 | .286 |
| Rain Rider | 5/1 | .167 |
| Sonus | 15/2 | .117 |
| Assessor | 14/1 | .067 |
| Mack The Knife | 14/1 | .067 |
| Shuailaan | 18/1 | .053 |
| Total of Chances | | 1.121 |

The chances of the seven runners added together do not total 1.000 because we are dealing with the *bookmaker's odds* not the *true odds*. The reason why the bookmaker stands to win in the long run is that the odds which he offers are, as we have noted already, weighted in his favour; and the extra .121 by which the chance total exceeds 1.000 represents the degree to which the odds in the Coalite St Leger were weighted in favour of the layer. If the chance total were less than 1.000 the odds would be in favour of the backer—a very rare occurrence. Successful bookmaking is founded on the principle that *at any one time* no backer is able to back all the competitors and be certain of a profit regardless of the result—a state of affairs known in the trade as 'over-round'.

What is the usual degree to which the bookmaker's prices are weighted against the backer? Well, a survey of over 2,000 races in 1992 gives an average chance total of 1.216. What does that mean? First of all, it would mean that any backer who used a random method of selection, taking all horses whose name ended with, say, the letter 'y', or picking them with a pin, or by some other silly, haphazard method, would get back £1,000 for every £1,216 staked, so would lose in the long run 216/1.216ths of his total investments—roughly 18p in the pound. Put in popular language we can say that in the contest between the bookmaker and the haphazard backer it is a little less than 5/4 on the bookmaker in one race. In the long run, of course, the haphazard backer has virtually no chance at all of coming out on top, and the figure 1.216 is a measure of the great handicap the clever backer has to overcome by skill if he is to make a profit out of backing horses.

## The Course Bookmaker

In practice, the Course Bookmaker does not expect remotely to approach this theoretical profit long term of 18p in the pound. For one thing, his clients are not all haphazard bettors of the pin-sticking variety, but a goodly number of well-informed backers who know as much about odds as the bookmaker does himself and who actually make a profit from their betting. For another, he cannot hope to lay all the runners in the correct proportion—as a rule laying all the runners in *any* sort of proportion is a feat in itself. Much of the time the bookmaker will succeed in attracting business for only part of the field and will have liabilities over one runner or more. The theoretical profit margin allows only for the sum of the prices to represent a percentage of over-round at the start, after which the bookmaker must feel his way according to the laws of supply and demand.

The Bookmaker's Profit Margin
(based on a survey of over 2,000 races in 1992)

| No of runners | Av Chance Totals | No of runners | Av Chance Totals |
|---|---|---|---|
| 2 | 1.037 | 12 | 1.244 |
| 3 | 1.076 | 13 | 1.271 |
| 4 | 1.099 | 14 | 1.304 |
| 5 | 1.109 | 15 | 1.284 |
| 6 | 1.126 | 16 | 1.336 |
| 7 | 1.139 | 17 | 1.345 |
| 8 | 1.164 | 18 | 1.349 |
| 9 | 1.174 | 19 | 1.392 |
| 10 | 1.199 | 20 + | 1.410 |
| 11 | 1.221 | | |

It must be remembered that 1.216 is an average figure. The chance total varies from race to race, and as our table shows there is a high degree of correlation between its size and the number of runners. In very small fields where all the runners are fancied and the bookmaker feels he can assess their chances accurately without being caught out, the chance total is regularly less than 1.100. In large fields, the size of the chance total tends to be exaggerated by the fact that bookmakers are chary of offering extreme odds about outsiders and prefer to lump them all together as, say, '25/1 others'. Bookmakers are not particularly concerned to try to attract money for outsiders, and prefer to have them running for the book. Consider, for example, these two races (*1992 Timeform Perspective* numbers are included for reference).

3624 Buckenham (S) Stakes (Newmarket)

|  | Odds | Chances |
|---|---|---|
| Soaking | 100/30 | .231 |
| Mam'zelle Angot | 4/1 | .200 |
| Greenwich Challenge | 7/1 | .125 |
| Nut Bush | 11/1 | .083 |
| Savings Bank | 12/1 | .077 |
| Clanrock | 12/1 | .077 |
| Sea Exhibition | 14/1 | .067 |
| 3 Horses at | 16/1 | .177 |
| 11 Horses at | 20/1 | .528 |
| 4 Horses at | 25/1 | .152 |
| 4 Horses at | 33/1 | .120 |
| Total of Chances |  | 1.837 |

907 Course Bookmakers Graduation (Pontefract)

|  | Odds | Chances |
|---|---|---|
| Star Family Friend | 4/9 | .692 |
| Whitley Gorse | 5/1 | .167 |
| Whisperdales | 5/1 | .167 |
| Total of Chances |  | 1.026 |

The Course Bookmakers Graduation Stakes (for two-year-olds) shows the bookmakers in their best light. Each of the three runners had run only once—successfully—yet the margin was only 2½% against the backer. In contrast, the Buckenham Selling Stakes, another two-year-old race, incidentally, represents the layers at their worst. Only four runners were quoted at more than 25/1 in a field of twenty-nine starters! Not many course bookmakers at Newmarket 'graduated' from Pontefract, apparently.

It is clear that the odds on offer in the Buckenham Stakes bear no relation whatever either to the true odds and chances of the runners, or to the actual business done by the layer, that is, to the state of his book. The chances of the twenty-six horses quoted from 11/1 to 33/1 represent 70% of the total chance, yet it must be extremely doubtful whether more than 10% of the bookmaker's field money came from these horses. Our guess is that 90% of the field money came from the first three in the betting, and with the favourite, ridden by Pat Eddery, going in, we should not be surprised if many bookmakers actually lost on the race! And deservedly so. In cases like this the bookmaker has become a gambler and given up any intention of trying to make a balanced book. He may have laid the first three favourites so that they are all losers for him in the hope that an outsider would be successful. Or he may have laid two of them, say Soaking and Mam'zelle Angot, to lose a lot of money, and kept Greenwich Challenge as light as possible in his book. In that event he would have become a backer of horses just as much as if he, like ourselves, had backed Greenwich Challenge, the Timeform top rated, in the ordinary way, but with the advantage over us that should the race go to an outsider, he would win and we should lose.

## Tote Betting

Unlike the bookmaker's percentage, the deduction the Tote makes from its pools is not governed by the size of the field, and currently stands at 16% from the win pool, 24% from the place pool, 26% from the Placepot and 29% from the Jackpot, Trio and Dual Forecast. If these figures are not off-putting enough, the backer faces additional deterrents of uncertainty over dividends and the inability most of the time for the Tote pools to absorb substantial bets. The Tote's win pool deduction equates to a chance total of 1.19 (100/84), a constant figure irrespective of the size of the field. So the successful Tote backer is more likely, generally, to find himself receiving better win odds (than SP) in races with eleven runners or more, and less likely, generally, in races of nine runners or fewer. Due to the high deduction from the place pool, for there to be any value in place-only betting one or two of the best-backed horses (or, better still, a short-priced favourite) needs to be out of the first three. In others words, the backer should consider betting place only on the Tote only when he has good reason to believe that at least one heavily-backed horse will be unplaced.

The backer can counter to some extent the uncertainty over the dividend he is likely to receive should his bet be successful by holding off until the runners are going into the stalls. Whether this tactic will work satisfactorily or not will depend on the number of other Tote punters doing the same thing. And there are bound to be quite a few. It would be unreasonable not to expect the bulk of late support to come for those runners whose projected dividends, displayed on TV monitors above the Tote windows, are greater than the odds known to be available with the course bookmakers. It is probably no accident that since the introduction and wide-spread use of these monitors, the superiority of Tote dividends over starting prices is confined largely to winners above the 10/1 mark. Winners ridden by popular jockeys can be expected usually to pay less (or less well, comparatively) on the Tote, whatever their SPs. Jackpots with huge amounts carried over regularly pay better than the accumulative SP odds, but are more the province of the fortune hunter than of the serious backer. So, too, is the Tote Placepot for all that it is less difficult to get up. The Placepot requires the backer to select a horse to be placed in each of the first six races. Dividends can be noticeably 'quirky' on occasion, and it makes sense for the Placepot backer to bet in anticipation of one or two favourites unplaced. In races with four runners or fewer the backer needs to select the winner.

## Ante-Post Betting

The easy general answer to the question whether or not the ordinary stay-at-home punter should bet ante-post is NO; for the reason that ante-post prices are always weighted more heavily against the backer than subsequent starting prices. Nowhere is this to be seen more clearly than in those races for which there has been no acceptance stage, big handicaps like the William Hill Cambridgeshire and the Tote Cesarewitch, for example. The first thing to be said about these particular two races—known popularly as the Autumn Double—is that they seem no longer to generate the lively ante-post interest they once did; whether because of the off-course betting tax; whether because rival firms are reticent when it comes to promoting interest in another company's races; or whether because any unexpected withdrawal of the top-weighted horses can bring unconsidered lightly-weighted horses 'into play' with the raising of the weights, we shouldn't care to say. What we can say is that in 1992 William Hill was the only firm consistently to advertise in the sporting press a comprehensive list of prices on these races from weight-publication date. An examination of Hill's opening lists published in *The Sporting Life* and *Racing Post* highlights the hazards which face the stay-at-home ante-post backer. Out of an entry of 115 for the Cambridgeshire, Hill quoted twenty-four horses on September 3rd for a chance total of .988; of those twenty-four, eighteen (75%) failed to get to the post come race-day, October 3rd. The Cesarewitch, with an entry of 72, wasn't much better: of the twenty-four horses Hill quoted on September 3rd for a chance total of 1.070, the twelve (50%) which did not get to the post six weeks later included the then favourite and one of the then co-second favourites. Clearly, the odds in both races were heavily weighted against the backer. We do not suggest that they were unduly bad, or that Hill (for our money the firm seen to be the most enterprising in the country when it comes to providing a comprehensive ante-post service) could fairly be blamed for not making them better. In considering only the horses that subsequently ran in these races the odds were decidedly in favour of the backer. This brings us to the crux of the matter. When the bookmaker, or perhaps one should say his ante-post manager, is compiling a list of prices against 115 and 72 horses entered in races over a month away, he does not know any more than anyone else does which of those horses will eventually run. But the owners and trainers and the stables' connections are in a very different position where their own horses are concerned. The ordinary backer at home may well back all sorts of horses, getting good prices about some, and inevitably losing money on a number of non-runners, but the big money of owners, trainers and professionals goes only on the certain runners. Consequently, if our friend the ante-post manager were to advertise, a month or so in advance of a big race, a list of prices which would be fair to the public in general, he would put his company at the mercy of those who bet only when they know. The comparative pittance he would get from the stay-at-home punter for the non-runners would not compensate him for the big bets laid at extravagant prices to the professionals. Therefore, when you examine ante-post prices with the aid of the Odds-Chances Table you should expect to find them weighted against the backer to a degree dependent on the type of race, the number of entries, whether or not there has been an acceptance stage, and how long there is to go to the date of the race.

The type of race is a factor because there is clearly much less doubt about stable intentions in classic races, pattern race events and championship races over the jumps, than there is in big handicap races like the Cambridgeshire and the Cesarewitch. Of the sixteen horses from an entry of thirty-one quoted by Hill in their advertisement a month before the 1993 Tote Cheltenham Gold Cup for a chance total of 1.366 (against an SP chance total of 1.238) eleven (68.75%) made it to the post and four others were withdrawn on the day. For the backer, come the day of the race the possibility of a big price about a fancied contender has dissipated to be replaced by the attraction of being able to bet at highly competitive prices, as the major firms, their cards well marked, trim their profit margins to lure customers into their shops. Applying the Odds-Chances Table to the prices offered by four leading bookmakers in their advertisements on the Friday and the Saturday (race-day) of the races in question in 1993 we obtain the following chance totals:-

| | Lincoln | | 2000 Guineas | |
| Bookmakers | Fri | Sat | Fri | Sat |
| --- | --- | --- | --- | --- |
| Dennis | 1.252 | 1.235 | 1.271 | 1.192 |
| Wm Hill | 1.239 | 1.184 | 1.256 | 1.204 |
| Surrey | 1.221 | 1.185 | 1.265 | 1.168 |
| Tote | 1.269 | 1.209 | 1.264 | 1.188 |
| SP Chance Total | | 1.249 | | 1.226 |

Note that in every case the prices on offer on the day of the race are better, significantly so most of the time, than those on offer the day before; and ultimately better than SP, too. Nor is there an appreciable difference in the profit margins between the Lincoln (a 24-runner handicap) and the Two Thousand Guineas (a 14-runner classic race).

Successful ante-post betting is all about timing. The backer who purposely delays supporting a horse ante-post at a price he considers to be attractive, until it has run its trial for the event in question, or until it races again, shows a lack of confidence in his judgement.

The vital conclusion one should draw from the foregoing is that it is foolish to bet ante-post unless

a) it is known that the horse is an intended runner, and

b) there are sound reasons for thinking the price will shorten.

## Trading In Odds

It is well said that a bet is never a good bet until it has been hedged. Trading In Odds is simply a more comprehensive phrase for a type of operation of which hedging is an example, and one of the attractions of ante-post betting is that it provides the enterprising course backer who is in a position to take bets (and a bookmaker, too, of course) with the opportunity of trading in odds. This is how it works. Let us imagine that a backer (or bookmaker) knowing a particular horse to be a certain runner for a big handicap over a month away, and having excellent reason to believe that it will be at much shorter odds on the day of the race than the 33/1 at which it stands when the lists open, accordingly, for trading purposes, books a bet of £20,000 to £600. When the price of the horse contracts to 16/1, he hedges the original bet by laying £5,000 to £300, so standing to win £15,000 for an outlay of £300—odds of 50/1 about a 16/1 chance! His trading so far has resulted in his *obtaining better value*. A day or two later he lays a further £5,000 to £300 off, leaving himself in the position of standing to win £10,000 if the horse is successful, with no possibility of loss if it is beaten. That is, he is on *something to nothing*. When the horse's price shortens further, he clinches matters by laying off a final £5,000 to £400, so finishing up in the highly desirable position of *standing to win both ways*; £5,000 if the horse wins, and £400 if it is beaten.

Once a backer has been lucky enough to secure a good bet at long odds about a horse which subsequently becomes a strong public fancy, the possibility of trading in odds always gives him the opportunity of

a) obtaining better value, or

b) being on something to nothing, or
c) standing to win both ways.

The desirability of beating the market is more evident when you consider it from this point of view. The snag for backers is that not many are in a position to hedge their bets in this way.

## Covering Bets

The practical use of the Odds-Chances Table which we have noted so far is the more or less negative one that it enables us to assess whether the market in a race gives the backer a reasonable chance, or is heavily in favour of the layer. If the former, we bet if so inclined; if the latter, we stand aside until the odds expand. Now for a more positive application of the Table.

For the sake of illustration, let us suppose that at the end of the 1992 Flat racing season, we wanted to speculate £100 on the outcome of the 1993 Ever Ready Derby. The horses in which we were interested, together with their prices on offer at the time and the equivalent chances as shown in the Table, were Tenby 7/1 (.125); Armiger 8/1 (.111); Barathea 25/1 (.038); Taos 25/1 (.038), and Fatherland 33/1 (.030). Instead of investing £20 on each, our intention was to arrange our stakes in such a way that

a) we stood to make the same clear profit should Tenby or Armiger win; and
b) we would break all square should one of the other three be successful.

That is to say, we required two straight bets clearing the same amount, and three covering bets. This is how we would have gone about it. First, the covering bets. Both Barathea and Taos were 25/1, the equivalent chance of .038, so on both we would have put .038 of £100—£4 to the nearest pound. Fatherland was 33/1 (.030)—so our stake on Fatherland would have been .030 of £100, i.e. £3. That would dispose of the three covering bets for an outlay of £11, each of which, if successful, would have returned us approximately the £100 with which we had started.

We would then have been left with £89 to split between Tenby and Armiger, so that we stood to clear the same amount whichever one of them should win. Tenby was 7/1 (.125) and

14

Armiger was 8/1 (.111), so we would have invested 125/236ths of £89 (£47 to the nearest pound) on Tenby and 111/236ths of £89 (£42 to the nearest pound) on Armiger. Where did we get the figure of 236 from? By adding together 111 and 125. In the form of a table, this would have been our completed business on the race:-

|  | Price | Stake | Win | Return | Profit |
|---|---|---|---|---|---|
| Tenby | 7/1 | £47 | £329 | £376 | £276 |
| Armiger | 8/1 | £42 | £336 | £378 | £278 |
| Barathea | 25/1 | £4 | £100 | £104 | £4 |
| Taos | 25/1 | £4 | £100 | £104 | £4 |
| Fatherland | 33/1 | £3 | £100 | £103 | £3 |
| Total Outlay | | £100 | | | |

Thus, we would have arranged matters so that we should have won just under £280 had either Tenby or Armiger been successful, and we would have saved our money had one of the other three won. The figures do not work out exactly as we staked to the nearest pound. It should be noted that the total obtained by adding the chances of the five horses together is .342. So, in backing them, we had in effect taken 66 to 34 (almost 2/1) that the winner would come from this group. Had we thought that this represented an unfair assessment, we should have been foolish to have backed them.

## Betting To Return An Equal Sum

We have seen that knowledge of the Odds-Chances Table is essential if the backer is to acquire a clear understanding of what it is he is trying to do. But this does not mean he should be prepared constantly to take his pocket calculator to the racecourse with him. Much of the time the arithmetic required of him will be fairly simple once he is used to it. Backing more than one horse to win an equal sum is an example. Let us suppose that a backer considers two horses, priced at 7/4 and 13/2 respectively, to represent value, and wishes to back them to return an equal amount, whichever of them wins. This is all he has to do:-

1) Back the horse with the *lower* odds, say £60 at 7/4 to win £105.
2) Add the £60 stake to the winnings to calculate the return— £165.

15

3) Divide the return by the odds + 1 of the other horse. Since 13/2 is 6.5/1, this would mean dividing £165 by 7.5 for an answer of 22. £22 at 13/2 returns £165.

In effect, the backer has combined two bets into one, as can be seen by adding the two together

Stakes £82 (£60 and £22), Return £165, Profit £83

The bet is therefore £82 to win £83—odds of around even money. This can be confirmed by checking with the Odds-Chances Table

7/4 (.364), 13/2 (.133), Total of Chances .497

To calculate the stake required on the horse at the longer odds using the Odds-Chances Table can fairly be said to be slightly more complicated, as it requires the backer ultimately to divide the smaller percentage .133 by the larger .364 (for an answer of 0.3654) and applying that answer to the original stake of £60 (for a final figure of £21.92). The figures do not work out exactly as we are dealing with decimals. Not that the backer would need to work out the stake as precisely as all that. He would know that 36.5% is a little more than one third, so that his stake on the horse at the longer odds should be a little over one third of £60. An understanding of how simply to calculate the relative stakes is very useful to the backer who has occasion to back two horses or more in a race, and who does not fancy one more than another relative to their prices.

## When To Bet Each-Way

The problem when to bet win only and when to bet each-way is a complex one to which no definite answer can be given. It is not possible to generalise and really each bet should be considered on its own merit. Nevertheless, there are certain broad considerations which are of great assistance in making a decision. We propose to indicate what those broad considerations are. In order to simplify matters, we shall consider only betting 1-2-3 in races where there are eight or more runners. Betting 1-2 in fields of 5, 6 or 7 runners is just the same in principle, so whatever conclusions are arrived at from a study of 1-2-3 place betting will have similar application to 1-2 betting.

Bookmakers at one time paid ¼ the odds 1-2-3. Now, except in handicaps where they pay ¼ the odds 1-2-3 in fields of 12 to 15 and ¼ the odds 1-2-3-4 in fields of sixteen plus, they pay ⅕ the odds 1-2-3.

We are apt to treat this fact as though it were one of the laws of nature: it is not a law of nature; it is a quite arbitrary arrangement adopted by the bookmaking fraternity in general. The first fact which must be accepted is that ⅕ *the odds a place is a custom for which there is no logical justification.* There is a justification of convenience, that is all. In a field of nine runners, if you bet 1-2-3 you are taking ⅕ the odds that your horse will finish in the first third of the field, but if you bet 1-2-3 in a field of 30 runners you are taking ⅕ the odds that it will finish in the first tenth of the field. It needs no argument to prove that the latter bet is much less favourable to the punter than the former. Nor that those numbers on the outer edge of the new scale, 7 and 15, offer the worst value, and those at the beginning, 8 and 16—one extra place for just one extra runner—offer the best value. But let us put the matter on a scientific basis by quoting actual odds and chances.

CASE 1 Open Market  –  Consider a race in which there are eight runners, each having exactly the same chance—i.e. there is no favourite and there are no outsiders. The chance, or probability, of each horse winning is ⅛ and the true odds against each should therefore be 7/1 (the bookmaker won't pay 7/1 each, since he has his profit to consider; but for the sake of argument let us assume that he will). Now if there are eight runners with equal chances, the chance of any horse being in the first three is ⅜ and the true odds against its being placed are 5 to 3 (8.33 to 5) against. The bookmaker, however, paying

| No. of Runners | True Win Odds | True Place Odds | Place Odds Paid | Percentage Difference |
|---|---|---|---|---|
| 8 | 7/1 | 8.33/5 | 7/5 | 16 |
| 9 | 8/1 | 10/5 | 8/5 | 20 |
| 10 | 9/1 | 11.66/5 | 9/5 | 23 |
| 12 | 11/1 | 15/5 | 11/5 | 27 |
| 15 | 14/1 | 20/5 | 14/5 | 30 |
| 18 | 17/1 | 25/5 | 17/5 | 32 |
| 21 | 20/1 | 30/5 | 20/5 | 33⅓ |
| 24 | 23/1 | 35/5 | 23/5 | 34¼ |
| 27 | 26/1 | 40/5 | 26/5 | 35 |
| 33 | 32/1 | 50/5 | 32/5 | 36 |

⅕ the odds 1-2-3 has to lay you to 7/5 a place. Thus, since 7/5 is smaller than 8.33/5, you are being paid under the odds. The table shows how the true place odds compare with the bookmakers' place odds with 8, 9, 10, 12, etc., runners all with equal chances. The figure in the final column shows the percentage disadvantage to the backers, of the odds paid compared with the true odds.

It can be seen at a glance that the bookmakers' arbitrary custom of paying ⅕ the odds 1-2-3 in non-handicap events is never in the favour of the backer and becomes more and more against him as the number of runners is increased. Now please don't jump to the hasty conclusion that one should never bet each-way. There is a great deal more to the question than that. The odds and percentages given in the table apply only in races in which all the runners have equal chances. If one horse is a hot favourite and the others range from, say 5/1 to 25/1, all the odds and chances in the table shown would, as we shall see in a moment, be changed. As we remarked before, each case has to be considered on its merits. Nevertheless, the table shown is not valueless, for it exposes the arbitrary nature of the ⅕ the odds 1-2-3 custom. This is important, for wherever accepted custom departs from true logic, there arises the opportunity for anyone with a little wit and understanding to make a profit. The profit can be made by realising when custom operates in your favour and taking advantage of it, and by keeping out of harm's way when custom operates against you. It also establishes the fact that *in general the greater the number of runners in a race the more the custom of paying ⅕ the odds a place operates in favour of the layer.* The popular idea that, in a big field you should back your fancy each-way is shown to be a fallacy at ⅕ the odds a place. The odds are against you, and mathematically it is better practice to back several horses to win.

CASE 2 A Short-Priced Favourite – Everyone knows that races of eight or more runners, all with equal chances, never occur in actual racing experience, so that the table is of theoretical rather than practical value. Let us, therefore, examine how matters stand with regard to place betting if, in a field of eight runners, one horse is an even-money favourite and the other seven are all outsiders with equal chances. The favourite's chance of winning is ½. The seven outsiders, therefore, have a ½ chance between them. So the chance of each outsider is 1/14, and the correct odds against each are consequently 13/1. We start with a field of eight runners, one at evens and the others at 13/1. Now so far as the favourite is concerned there are four possible results: it may be first, second, third or unplaced. Column 3 of the Table below gives the mathematical probability, expressed in decimal notation, of each possible result, and Column 4 the odds against its occurrence.

|  | Result | Probability | Odds Against |
|---|---|---|---|
| a) Favourite 1st | F x x | .500 | Evens |
| b) Favourite 2nd | x F x | .269 | 11/4 |
| c) Favourite 3rd | x x F | .135 | 13/2 |
| d) Favourite unplaced | x x x | .096 | 19/2 |

The reader will have to take the mathematics on trust, but he can be assured that the odds and chances are correct. We have the interesting fact that it is actually 19/2 against the favourite being unplaced, or, if you prefer it the other way round, it is 19/2 ON the favourite being in the first three. With the bookmaker, however, laying ⅕ the odds a place, it is only 5/1 ON, so if you back the even-money favourite for a place you will actually get *almost twice the true place odds*. That is an amazing fact, but more amazing still, the outsiders are also a proposition to back for a place (or each-way) for although the bookmaker lays you 13/5 for a place against any outsider, i.e. 2.60/1, the true place odds against each of these outsiders works out at only 2.40/1. It is, in fact, possible to bet on these outsiders so that you cannot lose. If you have £1 on each outsider for a place only at SP, at least two of your bets must be successful, for two outsiders must be placed. You get 2.60/1 each of them. Therefore you lose £5 and win £5.20. A clear profit of 20 pence (£3.80 if the favourite is unplaced) without any possibility of losing! No wonder bookmakers no longer as a general rule accept place-only wagers at fixed odds!

CASE 3 Two Short-Priced Runners  –  Now consider the case when there are two well-fancied horses in a field of eight runners. In order to make it more realistic let us give them names. Here is how the bookmakers bet: 4/6 Tenby, 5/1 Planetary Aspect, 25/1 The Six Others. The bookmakers would not in reality bet 25/1 bar two but for the sake of clarity let us stick to the true theoretical odds. The win prices offered by the bookmakers in our illustration are absolutely fair and allow for no profit by the layers. How are the place prices? Very definitely in favour of the backers, as the following shows:-

|  | True Win Odds | Place Odds Paid | True Place Odds |
|---|---|---|---|
| Tenby | 4/6 | 15/2 on | 26/1 on |
| Planetary Aspect | 5/1 | Evens | 9/4 on |
| The Six Others | 25/1 | 5/1 against | 7/2 against |

The place odds offered about the favourite are markedly in the backers' favour but for the purpose of a practical bet Plantetary Aspect presents an outstanding opportunity. The bookmakers are here caught up in their own ⅕ the odds-a-place custom to such a degree that an each-way bet on Planetary Aspect is, in racing parlance, money for nothing, as we are looking at a situation where the second favourite can be expected to win once for every twice that it is unplaced!

So far as The Six Others are concerned the place betting is also favourable to the backer, but we have to remember that the 25/1 win odds against the outsiders are the *true* odds. In practice the bookmakers would bet 12/1 others, with just under 5/2 a place, so that place betting on the outsiders would not be a proposition, as the true place odds are 7/2.

CASE 4 Three Short-Priced Runners – Except, marginally, in the case of The Five Outsiders, the place odds of each runner on the usual ⅕ the win odds basis are again greater than the true place odds, but to a much less marked degree than in the other examples. In the previous illustration Planetary Aspect, at 5/1, showed true place odds of as much as 9/4 on; Lyric Fantasy, at 5/1, here shows true place odds of only 11/8 on.

|  | True Win Odds | Place Odds Paid | True Place Odds |
|---|---|---|---|
| Sayyedati | 2/1 | 5/2 on | 9/2 on |
| Niche | 9/4 | 20/9 on | 4/1 on |
| Lyric Fantasy | 5/1 | Evens | 11/8 on |
| The Five Outsiders | 25/1 | 5/1 against | 21/4 against |

Thus when there are three fancied runners place betting does not favour the backer as much as when there are only two fancied runners. In fact, the more horses that are fancied out of eight the smaller becomes the advantage of betting each-way, until finally, when all eight horses are equally fancied, place betting ceases to offer any advantage at all to the each-way backer, as is shown in the table.

Well, finally, where exactly do we stand with regard to each-way betting at SP? It has been demonstrated that the bookmakers' custom of paying places at the rate of ⅕ the win odds is a makeshift and arbitrary arrangement with no scientific basis. In general each-way betting favours the bookmaker, but occasions arise when matters are definitely the other way about. To enable us to recognise them and act accordingly we have discovered three solid facts:-

1) The greater the number of runners the more place betting favours the bookmaker.
2) With an open market, place betting is on the side of the layer.
3) The presence of one or two short-priced horses in the field has the effect of making place betting highly advantageous to the backer.

The last of these conclusions is of the most practical value. Unfortunately, when you come to act upon it you will find your bookmaker reticent; and if you are unwise enough to persist in showing an each-way interest in races of the type covered by 3 with the same bookmaker, you run the risk of having the bet refused.

## Betting Each-Way In Handicaps

Betting each-way in handicaps is generally seen to be unattractive because of the competitive nature of these events. But, as our table shows, the bookmakers' practice of offering ¼ odds the first four in fields of 16 or more means that the odds the backer receives when his horse finishes in the first four are greater than the true chances of the horse's finishing in the first four, with the greatest advantage to the backer in percentage terms being in handicaps with precisely 16 runners. But we must remember our example is the hypothetical one where the odds reflect all the runners to have an equal chance. In practice the bookmakers would probably bet something like 12/1, and the true chance of the horse's finishing in the first four and the

| No of Runners | Place Odds Offered | True Win Odds | True Place Odds | Place Odds | % against % in favour |
|---|---|---|---|---|---|
| 5 | ¼ 1-2 | 4/1 | 1.5/1 | 1/1 | − 33 |
| 6 | ¼ 1-2 | 5/1 | 8/4 | 5/4 | − 37.5 |
| 7 | ¼ 1-2 | 6/1 | 10/4 | 6/4 | − 40 |
| 8 | ⅕ 1-2-3 | 7/1 | 8.3/5 | 7/5 | − 16 |
| 11 | ⅕ 1-2-3 | 10/1 | 2.7/1 | 2/1 | − 25 |
| 12 | ¼ 1-2-3 | 11/1 | 12/4 | 11/4 | − 8 |
| 15 | ¼ 1-2-3 | 14/1 | 8/2 | 7/2 | − 12.5 |
| 16 | ¼ 1-2-3-4 | 15/1 | 12/4 | 15/4 | + 20 |
| 20 | ¼ 1-2-3-4 | 19/1 | 16/4 | 19/4 | + 16 |
| 24 | ¼ 1-2-3-4 | 23/1 | 20/4 | 23/4 | + 13 |

odds received by the backer would be the same. Clearly, though, to the backer wishing to bet in a 16-runner (or more) handicap, if the win odds in his judgement are attractive, the place odds will be attractive. Nor should it be overlooked that most course bookmakers are prepared to bet each-way in handicaps but many are reluctant to do so in non-handicap events, so for a number of backers this is the one type of attractive each-way bet they will easily be able to place tax free.

## Each-Way Doubles

The fact that many bookmakers are prepared to offer bonuses to clients all of whose selections are successful in some types of multiple bets tells its own story. Not that there is anything theoretically wrong with multiple bets. The backer wins more when his selections are successful but wins less often. The rub is that as a rule the backer cannot be certain of the prices he would be getting, and therefore the value he would be receiving, on those of his selections in races much later than the time at which he places his bets. More to the point, he could achieve an admirable strike-rate of around 25%, with individual winners of 10/1 or more, and see his betting bank disappear into thin air. At odds of around 5/2, the 'yankee' bettor needs two winners just to break even, and sufficient resources to fund an operation that is likely to 'deliver' only once in a hundred and fifty bets. Without those resources, or a large slice of luck, he would be far better off in the short term betting in singles only, and letting the occasional three doubles and a treble that would have come his way slip through the net.

For the selective each-way backer who confines his multiple bets to 9/4 on place 'certainties' in those races which contain, or look reasonably sure to contain, one or two short-priced horses, the win element of his bet is not so critical. What matters is that his selections are placed. At ⅕ the odds a place, a double on two horses placed at true odds of 5/1 comes to 3/1, when the true place odds are around 11/10. Even at unattractive win odds of, say, 4/1, the place double returns a healthy well-over-value 9/4. In the event of the selective each-way backer finding four genuine 5/1 shots on the same day, the place element alone of a £1 each-way 'yankee' would yield a return of £72 for a total stake, win and place, of £22, against a return at true odds of £23.50.

## Betting Tax

The person who goes into a betting shop to place his bets, or who phones them through to his bookmaker, is rather like the trainer who habitually sends out his runners carrying overweight. He or she may still win, but where's the sense in making things more difficult than they need be? And if a backer is clever enough to win in the long run after paying a tax of 10% on his bets, he should be more than clever enough to appreciate that he should be operating on the racecourse, where bets with bookmakers are tax free. For the off-course backer the options are not to pay tax on with his bets but to have it deducted from his returns (if any) or to pay tax on so that any return is deduction free. The backer who elects not to pay tax on is saying to himself (whether he cares to admit it or not) that he is a loser and expects (or, at best, won't be surprised) to lose again. He is right not to pay tax on. The backer who includes the tax with his stake is being less pessimistic, and sees the sense in paying tax on the smaller amount going out rather than on the larger (hopefully) amount coming back in. His problem is how best to utilise the resources he has available. In other words, how to invest the money he is *prepared or can afford to part with* so it will do him the most good. If his limit is £100, he cannot afford to place a £100 bet and pay tax on top of it, as that would take him beyond his limit. His options, therefore, are to bet the full £100 and have tax deducted from the return, or to incorporate the tax into the bet so that the sum of the bet plus the tax he pays on it comes to £100. Let's see how this works.

| *Not Paying Tax* | | *Incorporating Tax* | |
|---|---|---|---|
| Sinclair Lad won 10/1 | | Sinclair Lad won 10/1 | |
| Stake | £100 | Stake | £90.91 |
| Win | £1,000 | Win | £909.10 |
| Return Before Tax | £1,100 | Return | £1,000 |
| Return After Tax | £990 | Profit | £900 |
| Profit | £890 | (£90.91+ 10% Tax) | £100 |

This proves that tax should be paid on, but should be incorporated *into* the intended stake, and *not* paid on top of it. The difference in our example is only £10, but in the long run small differences like this can add up to the big difference between winning and losing. Which is what counts. The stake when the backer was incorporating tax into the bet was, as you will have noticed, an impractical £90.91 (instead of £91) and was used for the purpose only of an accurate comparison.

Now let's go back to our imaginary bet on the 1993 Ever Ready Derby and see what happens to our calculations when, instead of placing our bets tax free on the racecourse with a bookmaker, we took our £100 (all we had to play with) into a betting shop. If we were to stake as we would on the racecourse, the 10% deducted from returns would result in our covering bets no longer doing the job they were calculated to do, and should one be successful, we should lose. As indeed we should lose if we were simply to reduce our stake on each horse by approximately 9/100ths to incorporate tax into our bet and keep the sum total of our investments to £100.

| | Odds | *Profit/Loss*<br>*Not paying Tax on* | *Profit/Loss*<br>*Paying Tax on* |
|---|---|---|---|
| Tenby | 7/1 | + £238.40 | + £241.82 |
| Armiger | 8/1 | + £240.20 | + £243.53 |
| Barathea | 25/1 | − £6.40 | − £5.46 |
| Taos | 25/1 | − £6.40 | − £5.46 |
| Fatherland | 33/1 | − £8.20 | − £7.78 |

What is important for us to remember when paying tax on with this particular type of bet is that although we are 'investing' £100, the amount we are actually putting to work for us is reduced—in the case of £100 by around £9—by the tax element. This £9 has to come off somewhere, but not from our covering bets, which are calculated as before; but from the £89 we have left to split between our two main bets, on Tenby and Armiger. Thus we invest 125/236ths of £80 (£42) on Tenby and 111/236ths of £80 (£38) on Armiger. So, after incorporating tax into our bet, our completed business on the race would read:

|  | Price | Stake | Win | Return | Profit |
|---|---|---|---|---|---|
| Tenby | 7/1 | £42 | £294 | £336 | £236 |
| Armiger | 8/1 | £38 | £304 | £342 | £242 |
| Barathea | 25/1 | £4 | £100 | £104 | £4 |
| Taos | 25/1 | £4 | £100 | £104 | £4 |
| Fatherland | 33/1 | £3 | £100 | £103 | £3 |

Total Outlay (£91 + 10% tax) £100 (approx)

The effect of incorporating tax into our investment is to reduce the odds at which we bet. We can see this in our example bet on Sinclair Lad at 10/1 where the backer received £1,000 (odds of 9/1) instead of £1,100. If the backer thought that Sinclair Lad represented value at 9/1, he was right to go ahead and back it. It is when the backer is betting, or thinking of betting, at odds much shorter than 10/1 that he must stop and ask himself whether it is worth it. At odds on, the difference in percentage terms between the actual odds and the odds the backer receives becomes a serious matter, and

Effective Returns at 10% Tax Prepaid

| Actual Odds | Effective Odds | Percentage Difference | Actual Odds | Effective Odds | Percentage Difference |
|---|---|---|---|---|---|
| 1/8 | 0.18/8 | 81.8 | 5/1 | 4.45/1 | 10.9 |
| 1/6 | 0.36/6 | 63.65 | 11/2 | 9.82/2 | 10.75 |
| 1/5 | 0.45/5 | 54.5 | 6/1 | 5.36/1 | 10.6 |
| 1/4 | 0.55/4 | 45.5 | 7/1 | 6.27/1 | 10.4 |
| 1/3 | 0.64/3 | 36.35 | 8/1 | 7.18/1 | 10.25 |
| 1/2 | 0.73/2 | 27.25 | 9/1 | 8.09/1 | 10.1 |
| 4/6 | 3.09/6 | 21.25 | 10/1 | 9.00/1 | 10 |
| 1/1 | 0.82/1 | 18.2 | 12/1 | 10.82/1 | 9.85 |
| 6/4 | 5.09/4 | 15.15 | 16/1 | 14.45/1 | 9.65 |
| 2/1 | 1.73/1 | 13.65 | 20/1 | 18.09/1 | 9.55 |
| 5/2 | 4.36/2 | 12.75 | 25/1 | 22.64/1 | 9.45 |
| 3/1 | 2.64/1 | 12.1 | 33/1 | 29.91/1 | 9.4 |
| 7/2 | 6.18/2 | 11.7 | 50/1 | 45.36/1 | 9.3 |
| 4/1 | 3.55/1 | 11.35 | 66/1 | 59.91/1 | 9.25 |
| 9/2 | 8.00/2 | 11.1 | 100/1 | 90.82/1 | 9.2 |

accelerates at an alarming rate beyond the point where there can possibly be any value to that at which the backer, theoretically, could actually back a winner and end up losing.

## Off-Course Betting

In practice, the bookmaker retains not just the 10% the off-course punter contributes towards tax and the levy (part of which goes straight into the bookmaker's pocket) but a further percentage to cover his expenses. The latest figures we have received through the International Racing Bureau show that backers get back in winnings 77% of money staked. In other words, they lose £23 out of every £100 they invest. To examine the effects of this 23% 'deduction', let's imagine a scenario where a syndicate of punters has clubbed together £1,000 to bet in betting shops on the eighteen races of a three-day meeting. The £1,000 is shared out equally among the syndicate members, and it is agreed that each of them is to bet the total amount of his full share, as he pleases, on the first race; after the first race the syndicate members are to meet, pool whatever

Effect of a 23% Deduction

|  | Race No | Stakes Invested | Winnings Received | Loss on Race | Cumulative Loss |
|---|---|---|---|---|---|
| First | 1 | £1,000 | £770 | £230 | £230 |
| Day | 2 | £770 | £592.90 | £177.10 | £407.10 |
|  | 3 | £592.90 | £456.53 | £136.37 | £543.47 |
|  | 4 | £456.53 | £351.53 | £105 | £648.47 |
|  | 5 | £351.53 | £270.68 | £80.85 | £729.32 |
|  | 6 | £270.68 | £208.42 | £62.26 | £791.58 |
| Second | 7 | £208.42 | £160.48 | £47.94 | £839.52 |
| Day | 8 | £160.48 | £123.57 | £36.91 | £876.43 |
|  | 9 | £123.57 | £95.15 | £28.42 | £904.85 |
|  | 10 | £95.15 | £73.27 | £21.88 | £926.73 |
|  | 11 | £73.27 | £56.42 | £16.85 | £943.58 |
|  | 12 | £56.42 | £43.44 | £12.98 | £956.56 |
| Third | 13 | £43.44 | £33.45 | £9.99 | £966.55 |
| Day | 14 | £33.45 | £25.76 | £7.69 | £974.24 |
|  | 15 | £25.76 | £19.84 | £5.92 | £980.16 |
|  | 16 | £19.84 | £15.28 | £4.56 | £984.72 |
|  | 17 | £15.28 | £11.77 | £3.51 | £988.23 |
|  | 18 | £11.77 | £9.06 | £2.71 | £990.94 |

they have, share it out again, and each once more to bet his full share, as he pleases, on the second race, and so on. Assuming the backers, as a whole, are neither more nor less fortunate than normal, but they lose 23% of what they bet, how do they fare, and how long will it be before they are broke? Our table shows what happens.

After only six races the syndicate punters have lost nearly 80% of their starting capital; at the end of the second day, after twelve races, they have lost over 95% of it; and at the end of the three-day meeting, after eighteen races, they have less than £10 remaining. To all intents and purposes, they are broke. The original £1,000 has been virtually extinguished—more than 99% lost. We may say, therefore, that on the evidence of the latest figures we have to hand, of a reported 23% deduction made from the stakes of backers betting off course, the extinction point (where less than 1% of the original stakes remains) for re-bet money is reached after eighteen events.

£1,000 Bet and Re-Bet to Extinction

| Total Take-Out | Money 99% lost after | Total Take-Out | Money 99% lost after |
|---|---|---|---|
| 12% | 37 bets | 22% | 19 bets |
| 13% | 34 bets | 23% | 18 bets |
| 14% | 31 bets | 24% | 17 bets |
| 15% | 29 bets | 25% | 17 bets |
| 16% | 27 bets | 26% | 16 bets |
| 17% | 25 bets | 27% | 15 bets |
| 18% | 24 bets | 28% | 15 bets |
| 19% | 22 bets | 29% | 14 bets |
| 20% | 21 bets | 30% | 13 bets |
| 21% | 20 bets | | |

It should be stressed that the exercise is an artificial one. Backers don't stake everything they have every time they bet, nor do they bet in every race. At the end of every race meeting there will always be a minority of backers who have come out as winners. It is also true that backers who bet race by race in 'singles' don't actually lose 23% per race. The average figure is as high as 23% only because much of the money bet off-course is on multiple bets, from which the bookmaker's profit is much higher. In our illustration had our syndicate been operating on the racecourse with a loss, say, of 13%, they would have returned home with £81.50, less expenses: they could have gone on betting for sixteen more races. Had they been betting on a racecourse in America, where punters reportedly lose, on average, 20% of their investment capital, their dollar bank would have held out for a total of twenty-one races.

We have seen that the effect of tax on the off-course backer is effectively to reduce the odds at which he bets. As successful betting is all about getting the *best* of the odds, and few professionals make 10% on turnover in the long run, it does not add up that well over 90% of money speculated with bookmakers on horse racing in this country should be speculated off course. But few of us are in the happy position of being able to place all our bets on the racecourse, or to have our bets placed on the racecourse for us. And even those of us who are in that position, bet off course when it suits us to do so. How then does the off-course backer make the best of what is, in all honesty, a bad job? Not by reducing his tax burden by betting in doubles, trebles and accumulators. The backer who confines his betting operation to the placing of multiple bets dances to the bookmaker's tune—with the probability that his money will jingle out of his pocket straight into the bookmaker's lap. Nor by the placing of win bets at prices generally so short that any value to be had in them is largely eaten up by the tax element. But by the judicious selection of value win 'singles' and value each-way singles and doubles in races on which bookmakers are unlikely to advertise a willingness to bet each-way on the racecourse. On the subject of 'value' betting, when the backer considers the price of a horse to be attractive, generally speaking he should back it, rather than hang on in the hope that it will become more attractive still. Unless he is way out on a limb, chances are other backers will think the same as he does and the price of the horse will go the 'wrong' way. And if he hasn't bet his limit and the price of the horse does happen to lengthen, he can always back it again. An exception to this generalisation is the opening show, when prices tend to be contracted. Subscribers to reputable betting services, however, should always consider taking 'first show' in the knowledge that a considerable amount of money is likely to be invested on the horse they have been advised to back.

For those backers who prefer to see odds as percentages the approximate percentages of the odds most frequently used are tabled below. By referring to them the backer will be able quickly to assess the margin against him and so judge the likelihood of prices lengthening, given that the bookmaker's percentage is equivalent usually to around two points per runner.

Odds as Percentages

| On | Odds | Against | On | Odds | Against |
|----|------|---------|----|------|---------|
| 50 | Evens | 50 | 83 | 5/1 | 17 |
| 52 | 11/10 | 48 | 86 | 6/1 | 14 |
| 56 | 5/4 | 44 | 89 | 8/1 | 11 |
| 60 | 6/4 | 40 | 91 | 10/1 | 9 |
| 64 | 7/4 | 36 | 92 | 12/1 | 8 |
| 67 | 2/1 | 33 | 93 | 14/1 | 7 |
| 69 | 9/4 | 31 | 94 | 16/1 | 6 |
| 71 | 5/2 | 29 | 95 | 20/1 | 5 |
| 73 | 11/4 | 27 | 96 | 25/1 | 4 |
| 75 | 3/1 | 25 | 97 | 33/1 | 3 |
| 78 | 7/2 | 22 | 98 | 40/1 | 2 |
| 80 | 4/1 | 20 | 98 | 50/1 | 2 |
| 82 | 9/2 | 18 | 99 | 100/1 | 1 |

It would be nice to think that the off-course backer has something going for him. And he has. The early-betting races. Each day prices for a few specially selected races (usually competitive handicaps) are released from around 9.30 am; and prices for important races covered by television are often advertised on the day of the race in the national press. These latter events come under the scrutiny of *Pricewise* in the *Racing Post*, an excellent service to backers which saves them time and trouble by collating the advertised prices in the one easy-to-refer-to little table: with informed comment thrown in. Suffice to say, any value to be found in these events, and in the 'early betting' races, will have been snapped up long before the bettor on the racecourse has a chance to get in on the act. But it must be remembered, we are talking here of a minority of races. The sensible advice to readers anxious to get the most from their betting is to go racing.

# Spread Betting

Spread betting is a relatively new concept, as yet not taken up by the major firms. What sets it apart from 'normal' betting as we know it are the following factors.

1) The backer has the chance of match betting, on a lengths start basis, within a race.

2) The result determines the amount staked when the backer loses, and the amount won when the backer wins (therefore all bets must necessarily be on credit).

To illustrate, we will look at the 1¼m85y 1993 Juddmonte International Stakes at York from the point of view of a 'match' between Sabrehill and White Muzzle, the latter getting a length start, displayed thus—Sabrehill/White Muzzle 0–1. Let's imagine that we decide to oppose White Muzzle on the grounds that the distance is likely to prove too sharp for him, and accordingly back Sabrehill to beat him at £20 per length. As we can see, Sabrehill finished eight and a half lengths ahead of White Muzzle, seven and a half lengths *more* than the length start he was conceding. Therefore our profit on the bet is 7½ × £20; ie £150. Had White Muzzle finished eight and a half lengths *ahead* of Sabrehill, we should have *lost* £190 (8½ × £20 plus the length start). The fact that neither horse won the race is irrelevant. Had one of the two horses not finished (or been soundly beaten), a limit of twelve lengths (fifteen lengths over the jumps) would be imposed.

| | | | |
|---|---|---|---|
| 1502 | EZZOUD (IRE) *MRStoute* 4-9-6 (v) WRSwinburn (3) .................28/1 | 1 | |
| 2247 | SABREHILL (USA) *HRACecil* 3-8-12 MRoberts (4)...................7/4f | 1½ | 2 |
| 2277 | SPARTAN SHAREEF (IRE) *CEBrittain* 4-9-6 RCochrane (8).......50/1 | 5 | 3 |
| 2172 | Revelation (IRE) *RHannon* 3-8-12 AdaCruz (10) ..........................9/1 | 1½ | 4 |
| 2393 | White Muzzle *PWChapple-Hyam* 3-8-12 JReid (5).....................2/1 | 2 | 5 |
| 1946 | Blues Traveller (IRE) *BWHills* 3-8-12 MJKinane (7) ..................15/1 | 1½ | 6 |
| 2393 | Tenby *HRACecil* 3-8-12 PatEddery (2)........................................15/2 | nk | 7 |
| 1620 | Guado d'Annibale (IRE) *ARenzoni,Italy* 4-9-6 DHolland (1) .......66/1 | 2 | 8 |
| 2393 | Environment Friend *NCWright* 5-9-6 (v) GDuffield (9).............28/1 | 5 | 9 |
| 2486 | Alhijaz *JLDunlop* 4-9-6 WCarson (6)..........................................20/1 | 15 | 10 |
| 1976 | Red Bishop (USA) *JHMGosden* 5-9-6 LDettori (11)...................14/1 | 8 | 11 |

There is far more to spread betting than our simple illustration allows. Performance Betting, for example, enables the astute backer, in effect, to lay a 'bad' favourite. In a nutshell, the spread bettor is an 'investor', with the facility to 'trade' according to the wind. For the bettor of sound judgement, spread betting is an opportunity to exercise his judgement to greater effect; for others it is just another conveyance along the same old bumpy road. The advantages to the backer over normal betting are that the spread bookmaker works to lower limits and pays the tax. Bookmakers are not charity institutions. Those who introduced spread betting did so on the advice that it would prove to be a money-spinner for them. If this expectation is not realised, they will abandon it.

## Staking Systems Exposed

If anyone reading this section hopes to find in it details of the perfect system which will put him on the way to a fortune by the mere expedient of manipulating stakes, he is doomed to disappointment. But he will be well advised to continue reading it, all the same, for it is to him who has hopes of this kind that it is particularly addressed. We shall disillusion him without further ado. There is no perfect staking system, and there can be no perfect staking system. Furthermore, there is not, and cannot be, any staking system which possesses even the most infinitesimal *intrinsic* advantage over pure, ordinary, unadulterated level stakes.

Sequences – Most staking systems one comes across are based upon a misunderstanding of sequences. If an unbiased coin is tossed six times, and each time it comes down heads, it is still exactly an even-money chance that it will come down heads on the seventh time. This is ordinary common sense. If a jockey has ridden 50 consecutive losers, he is not one whit more likely to ride a winner next time he rides. If the favourite has failed in each of the first five races of the day, that does not mean the last favourite is any more (or less) likely to win. If trap 3 has not provided a winner from 50 races, that is not the slightest justification for a belief that it will now be profitable to start backing that trap number. Undoubtedly, though, there are many people who go racing who believe the reverse of these facts to be true.

The 'Law of Averages' – Their belief in these fallacies is based upon what they think is the *Law of Averages*. They argue because it is a 50/50 chance that a tossed coin will come down heads, that therefore if you go on tossing it often enough you will get exactly 50% heads and 50% tails. They are wrong. The word 'exactly' makes the contention false. If it read 'the longer you go on tossing the coin the nearer you will get to 50% heads' it would be a perfectly true statement of fact. They proceed to deduce that after 200 tosses of a coin have provided 108 heads the next 200 are likely to provide 108 tails because things have to be evened up in the long run. They are wrong again. The so-called 'law of averages' says nothing of the sort. In fact, there is no such thing as a 'law of averages'. There is only a *Law of Great Numbers*. We hope the reader will forgive our going further into this business before we return to staking systems proper, because it is of the utmost importance that it should be understood.

If you toss a coin 100 times it is an even chance that you will get less than 56.75% of either heads or tails; if you toss it 1,000 times it is an even chance that you will get less than 52.133% heads or tails; and if you toss it a million times the odds are that you will not get more than 50.0674% heads or tails. Thus it is perfectly true that the more trials you make of a chance event the nearer the result approaches to the true theoretical probability. The popular way of mis-stating this fact is to say that the effect of luck diminishes as the number of the events is increased. Whatever may be meant by 'the effect of luck', this popular way of expressing a statistical fact is admissible only if 'the effect of luck' is understood as applying to the *percentage* result. It is because people take it as applying to the actual numerical result that their conclusions are so dangerously false.

Let us make the difference clear by returning to the 100, 1,000 and 1,000,000 tosses of a coin. In 100 tosses it is evens that you will get not more than 56.75% heads or tails, *i.e.* between 44 and 56 heads; in 1,000 tosses it is evens that you will get not more than 52.133% heads or tails, *i.e.* between 479 and 521 heads. Thus on 100 tosses the chances are that you may be only six out either side of the theoretical 50/50, but on 1,000 tosses the chances are that you may be 21 out. The *percentage* probable error is *smaller*, but the actual *numerical* probable error is *larger*. If you go on to a million tosses the odds are that you will get a 50.0674% result, *i.e.*, only .0674% different from the 'true' result. But .0674% of a million is 674,

| No. of Tosses | *Probable %*<br>*Result*<br>*Heads or Tails* | *Probable*<br>*Numerical Error*<br>*Heads or Tails* |
|---|---|---|
| 100 | 43.25–56.75 | 6 Out |
| 1,000 | 47.87–52.13 | 21 Out |
| 1,000,000 | 49.93–50.07 | 674 Out |

32

so your actual numerical result may well be as many as 674 out either way. Put these figures side by side and you will recognise the fallacy in the popular idea of the so-called law of averages.

Thus it is actually true that the more tosses you make the *more* (in number, *not* percentage) you are likely to be out from the theoretical 50/50 figure. Just the opposite of what many people think.

What we have just demonstrated is the mathematical result of the observed fact that WHAT HAS GONE BEFORE HAS, IN MATTERS OF CHANCE, NO INFLUENCE WHAT-EVER ON WHAT MAY HAPPEN AFTERWARDS.

We can now return to a brief examination of the fundamental types of staking system plans.

'Step-In' and 'Step-Out' Systems  –  It is immediately obvious that all systems which ask you to wait until a certain sequence of results has occurred, and then step in and start betting, can be consigned to the dustbin right away. No matter whether they are systems of following newspaper writers' tips after they have given, say, five consecutive losers, or whether they involve backing favourites after so many consecutive favourites have gone down, or anything of this type. They are all equally worthless, because they are all based upon the same false assumption. This applies to the 'step-out' systems which advise you to stop betting, or reduce your stakes, after so many consecutive winners.

You often hear it said that luck runs in patches, a good patch being followed by a bad one. Of course! But you can't make use of this phenomenon for betting purposes, since it is impossible to forecast when a good or a bad patch will start or when it will finish.

Increasing Stakes after a Loser  –  The big majority of staking systems belong to this class, and the basic plan from which they are all derived may be represented as follows:— *1 point for the first bet; increase 1 point after each loser; after a winner revert to the 1 point and repeat.* The fact is that all systems of increasing stakes after losers depend for their success or failure upon the sequence in which the winners and losers occur in the series of bets to which they are applied. If the winners are well spaced out with a string of losers preceding each winner they are successful; but if the winners occur consecutively, or bunched together, they are unsuccessful. For example, take a series of twenty bets, fifteen losers and five winners at Evens, 2/1, 3/1, 4/1 and 5/1. On level stakes this series of bets leaves the backer all square whatever the order in which the winners and losers occur. But on the basic staking plan given above, increasing one point after a loser and reverting to the minimum one point after a winner, the profit or loss result depends entirely upon the way you arrange the winners and losers. On this sequence:—

L.L..L.L.3/1,L.L.L.5/1,L.L.2/1,L.L.L.4/1,L.L.L.Evens

the result is a profit of 30 points. But bunching the winners together in this fashion:—

L.L.L.L.L.L.L.L.Evens,5/1,4/1,L.3/1,2/1,L.L.L.L.L.L

results in a loss of 32 points.

Decreasing Stakes after a Loser  –  The basic plan is something like this: Bet in 1 point stakes until you strike a winner, then jump your stake to 4 points (for example); decrease 1 point after each loser until you reach the minimum 1 point stake, with which you continue until another winner jumps it to 4 points again; always bet in 4 point stakes after a winner. The assumption behind the plan is that when you are 'in form' you will be frequently using 4, 3 or 2 point stakes, but when you are 'out of form' you will be using the minimum 1 point stake. Naturally the plan is successful when the winners are bunched together and unsuccessful when they are isolated. Taking exactly the same sequences as before we have the following results:—

L.L.L.L.3/1,L.L.L.5/1,L.L.2/1,L.L.L.4/1,L.L.L.Evens

shows a loss of 21 points, whereas the sequence

L.L.L.L.L.L.L.L.Evens,5/1,4/1,L.3/1,2/1,L.L.L.L.L.L

shows a profit of 30 points.

It is clear that these two staking plans, increasing after a loser and decreasing after a loser, contradict one another. They cannot both be right, for if the sequence of results over a long period suits the first plan it will not suit the second, and *vice-versa*. In practice everyone gets sequences of results which are, in the long run, of both kinds, and consequently, like step-in and step-out systems, both plans are neither better nor worse than ordinary level stakes. There are many variants upon them, but they all come to the same thing in the end.

It should be noted in passing that you cannot compare a 10-11-12 . . . . . point staking system with a 1-2-3 . . . . . point plan, or with level stakes, merely by looking at the final points results. The 10-11-12 . . . . . point method will naturally give an exaggerated final figure because the average stake employed is higher. For example 1-2-3-4 . . . . . staking applied to this series of results: L.L.L.2/1,10/1, L., shows an apparent profit of 11 points, but the real profit is only 5½, since the average stake used is 2 points—a worse result than level staking, which shows 8 points profit on 1 point per bet. *The true result of a staking plan is obtained by dividing the final profit (or loss) by the average stake employed.*

Every tipster, no matter how bad, has a winning run sooner or later, and it is greatly to his advantage to magnify the profit on the period as much as possible. Consequently tipsters are very fond of staking systems. When a tipster advertises that from May 31st his selections showed, on his own special staking plan, a profit of 200 points, he really tells you nothing at all, for his *true* profit may be only 10 or 20 points. But it looks very attractive in print, and punters will be taken in by it.

Proportionate Staking – Speaking generally, practically all staking plans are derived from one or other of the basic methods already disposed of (perhaps from a combination of two or three of them), but there is one further plan which ought to be mentioned: that is, the *arrangement by which one always bets with a certain proportion of one's capital.* For example, the backer starts with a bank of, say, £20, and proceeds to bet with, say, ⅟₂₀ of his capital. His first stake is therefore £1. If his bet loses, his bank is reduced to £19, and his second stake is ⅟₂₀ of £19, *i.e.*, 95p. If this loses also, his third stake is ⅟₂₀ of the £18.05 left, *i.e.*, 90p to the nearest penny, and so on. If the first bet had won at, say, 10/1 the £10 profit would have been added to the original £20, bringing the bank up to £30, and the second stake would have been ⅟₂₀ of £30, *i.e.*, £1.50.

One need not adjust the stake after every bet. The principle is exactly the same if one adjusts the stake according to the size of the bank after every ten bets, or after every week, month or year, as one pleases.

If a backer loses on level stakes this proportionate method of betting won't help him. In theory a losing backer can never lose the whole of his bank, since his stakes get smaller as the size of his bank decreases, but in practice the stakes eventually get too small to invest, and he has to start with a fresh bank. But if the backer wins on level stakes, proportionate betting increases his winnings, because the more cash he has in hand the bigger his bets. The winning backer is in the position of a successful businessman who is pushing ahead with the expansion of his business by putting all his profits back into it. One should also note that because all the betting profits go back into the betting bank the winning backer makes no personal profit at all until he ceases using the method.

In reality it is not a staking system at all, in the true sense of the phrase. It is merely ordinary level stake betting, in which one periodically changes one's stake to suit the size of one's bank. That's all there is to it.

When Staking Plans may be Justified – It should be clear now that it is impossible to invent a staking plan which has any *intrinsic* advantage over ordinary level stakes. All plans must depend for their success on winners and losers occurring in the kind of sequence which suits them. Therefore the only time you are justified in using a staking plan is when you have some sound logical reason for expecting one kind of winner-loser sequence rather than another. Consider the following:-

Suppose you decide to back every Big Handicap winner on each of its next three outings. You might argue in either of two ways. (a) You might contend that, having won a big handicap with the horse, the stable is likely to give it one or two easy races before going for the gloves again. If you adopt this line of argument you would be right to follow each horse on 1-2-3 stakes, on the ground that is is more likely to win on its third outing than on its first. (b) On the other hand you might argue that, having won a big race and proved it to be at the top of its form, the horse is likely to win again at the first time of asking, and that if it doesn't manage to win first time it is less likely to do so on the second and third outings, as probably by then it will have passed its peak of fitness. If you adopt this line of argument you would have logical grounds for backing each horse in 3-2-1 stakes.

In practice the success or failure of your method—*i.e.*, its advantage or disadvantage as compared with level 2 point stakes—depends on the rightness or wrongness of your basic assumption. Neither staking plan of itself possesses any intrinsic advantage.

Questions to ask Oneself – We have now reviewed the fundamental types of staking plans, and on the basis of these types the reader ought to be in a position to assess practically all the systems which it may fall to his lot to examine. He has to ask himself two questions about any system.

1) Is the staking based on an attempt to apply the 'law of averages' or other mathematical trickery? If the answer is YES, no further consideration is needed. The plan should go into the fire immediately. If the answer is NO, you then ask:-

2) What is the assumption on which the staking is based? And also, is this assumption sound? The latter question can be decided only (a) by applying your general knowledge of racing, or (b) a *very* long practical test.

Whatever you do, *never* judge a staking plan on the profit which it shows over a series of bets selected by the man who advocates the plan; not even after you have turned the profit into true profit by dividing by the average stake used. It is a favourite trick of tipsters and system-mongers to invent the kind of staking plan which fits the results after the results are known. There is no guarantee that it will also fit results in the future. Always judge a staking plan on fundamental basic principles.

## The Betting Bank

Having stated that there is no staking system intrinsically superior to level staking, we must address ourselves to the problem: 'What can be regarded as a bank of a satisfactory size for a backer to operate on?' This is a difficult question to answer, but in the hope of casting a little light upon it let us first examine the mathematics of consecutive losers.

Consecutive Losers – The first obvious fact is that the chance of a backer's having, say, 20 consecutive losers in a given period depends (a) upon the number of bets he makes in that period, and (b) upon his skill in selecting winners, *i.e.*, upon the percentage of winners which he is able to maintain in the long run. The higher a backer's percentage of winners the longer the odds against his having a sequence of, say, 20 consecutive losers in a given number of bets. Below we give a table which shows the frequency with which one can expect runs of 10, 15, 20, 25 or 30 consecutive losers to occur with backers who are able over a long period to average 50%, 40%, 33⅓%, 30%, 25%, 20% and 16⅔% winners.

Mean Intervals between Occurrences of Losing Runs

| win prob | av no of bets between starts of losing runs length at least | | | | |
|---|---|---|---|---|---|
| | 10 | 15 | 20 | 25 | 30 |
| 0.500000 | 2048 | 65536 | 2097152 | — | — |
| 0.400000 | 413 | 5317 | 68378 | 879344 | 11308430 |
| 0.333333 | 173 | 1314 | 9976 | 75753 | 575246 |
| 0.300000 | 118 | 702 | 4178 | 24856 | 147890 |
| 0.250000 | 71 | 299 | 1261 | 5315 | 22399 |
| 0.200000 | 47 | 142 | 434 | 1323 | 4039 |
| 0.166667 | 37 | 92 | 230 | 572 | 1424 |

This assumes that the indicated win probability remains the same for each bet

The table is quite simple to interpret. The first line tells us that a backer who averages 50% winners can expect a run of 10 consecutive losers to start after an average of 2,048 bets; a run of 15 consecutive losers to start after an average of 65,536 bets; and so on. The other lines are interpreted in the same way.

The Losing Run  –  Unfortunately, the number of consecutive losers which we are likely to get in a given period does not settle the question of what is a satisfactory bank. What we are concerned with is not the backing of a number of consecutive losers, but the losing of a number of points on any sequence of bets. For a bank to be satisfactory it has to be large enough to meet the worst losing sequence we are likely to get whether that sequence includes winners or not. And this depends not only upon the percentage of winners we can maintain, but also upon the average price of these winners.

Other things being equal, a method which gives 50% winners requires a much smaller bank than one which gives 25% winners. But other things are not equal. What really decides matters is the *rate of profit achieved*, not the probability of a given number of consecutive losers.

The Personal Element – The final aspect of the question of what is a satisfactory bank is the personal one. A bold and adventurous punter, who is prepared to take a chance on a losing run coming at the beginning, will operate from a much smaller bank than would a cautious man or woman, who prefers to allow for the worst to happen right at the start. It is all a question of temperament. The bold and adventurous punter will be all right so long as the losing run does not come at the beginning. Our advice is to be cautious, and to bet within your means.

To anyone who achieves a high rate of profit with 25% winners, a 10 point bank, *i.e.* betting in £10 stakes on a capital of £100, or to £200 stakes on a capital of £2,000, will give a reasonable degree of safety to start with. A bank, however, which is intended to be *permanent, i.e.,* which is not to be strengthened by adding to it from future winnings, ought to be considerably larger than one which is merely regarded as safe to *start* with. A 20 point bank will give a very high degree of permanent safety to a punter who achieves a high rate of profit with 25% winners.

## The Bets To Seek

We have stated that there is absolutely no advantage to be obtained from manipulating stakes according to winner-loser sequences. But this does not mean that one should bet always in level stakes. Indeed this is theoretically quite wrong.

In the first place, if a bet is a bet for 10p it is a bet for a million pounds. A bet, a worthwhile bet that is to say, is one which is made at odds greater than they should be. A bet at 2/1 about a horse whose 'true odds' should be 'evens' is a very worthwhile bet. Such bets must necessarily show a profit in the long run. These are the bets to seek. If you can get 3/1 or 4/1 about a horse that should be 6/4 it's a Bet with a capital B. Whether you bet in pence, pounds or thousands, it's a Bet.

Differential Staking – What, then, should determine the stake you are entitled to have on a horse? One answer is the size of your bank balance—your financial resources. A millionaire would be entitled to hazard far more than a man with a few hundreds in the bank. So the first point is that your stakes must be related to your resources, which should be *big enough to enable you to stand a run of ill fortune, when even the best of good things get beaten.*

In the second place it is also clear that a backer is entitled to bet more on a true even-money chance than he would be on a true 7/1 chance. The former will win in the long run one race in every two: the latter in the long run only one race in every eight. So you are entitled to have far more on even-money chances than you are on 7/1 chances.

We won't pursue the matter. Take it from us, not only must the general level of your betting be governed by your financial resources, but the actual size of your bets on individual horses should be related to their true chances of winning against the odds you are receiving. This is what is meant by differential staking.

'And so, gentlemen, I move that a special committee be appointed to consider what measures may be taken to deal with the menace of Timeform!'

# Betting The Timeform Way:

## In Practice

For the backer to make a success of his betting he must discipline himself to bet only when he considers the odds to be attractive, that is to say, only when the odds available are greater than his assessment of the true (or fair) odds yet are at the same time short enough to give him reasonable prospects of a return on his investment. Assessing the true odds in events of pure chance, such as the spin of a roulette wheel or the fair toss of a coin, is a simple matter. Whether the wheel is spun slowly or whether it is spun quickly, whether the coin is allowed to fall to the ground or whether it is caught in one hand and turned over on to the back of the other, the odds never vary. They are immune to outside influence. Assessing the true chances of the contestants in a horse race—the outcome of which is influenced by outside factors such as the distance of the race, the going on which it is run, the pace at which it is run, the course over which it takes place, the effect of the draw, and so on, as it is by the relative merits of the runners at the weights—is another matter entirely. And if the problems posed by outside factors are not enough, there are those posed by the runners themselves. One may be wearing blinkers for the first time; one may have been running successfully abroad; one, with a good chance on its best form, may have been off the course for some time through injury; another may be a well-bred newcomer from a top stable; another may have shown vastly improved form in blinkers last time out but for reasons best known to its connections is not wearing blinkers on this occasion; another, with no measurable form but from a 'warm' stable, may have caught everyone's eye (except those of the stewards) on its previous outing: yet another, perhaps the form horse of the race, may have run unaccountably badly on its most recent appearance; while another, also with a good chance on its best form, may be inconsistent and unreliable; another may have been transferred recently from a well-known stable to a little-known one, or vice-versa; and yet another may have won its only race very easily but at a lower level. Problems like these confront the backer every day of the week, if not all at

41

once in the same race, and even Einstein would have trouble in coming up with a fair price. So, if some 'genius' you have the misfortune to know solved a problem you found too difficult to contemplate, and to rub it in is making a poor job of keeping quiet about it, there's no reason to be downhearted. Wise backers know when to stay out and you will be in good company.

Recognising value in the odds is a matter of judgement, not of mathematics. And it is a matter of judgement borne of experience, long and bitter. This last section is devoted to helping the backer who subscribes to the Timeform service make those decisions upon which the success of his betting depends.

## Timeform Ratings

Timeform's 'two top-rated' win around half of all races. The two most important factors (aside from the skill of Timeform's handicappers) influencing the 'performance' of the ratings are the frequency of small fields and the ratio of handicaps to non-handicap events. The less competitive the race, the easier it is generally to pinpoint the likely winner. When Timeform's top-rateds get beaten, they do so for a variety of reasons, one of which is that they should not have been top-rated in the first place. Timeform ratings enjoy a world-wide reputation for their accuracy and impartiality, and have done so since they were first published in 1948. But they are not gospel. Timeform is frequently wrong about horses, giving them ratings that are too high or too low. This is in the nature of things—an occupational hazard. Handicapping horses is no more than an expression of opinion.

Many other Timeform top-rateds get beaten because one or more of their opponents improves past them. In non-handicap events identifying top-rateds 'at risk' is a simple matter of referring to the TRW figures, printed in the Timeform Race Cards and Race Ratings Booklets. TRW figures are the age and weight-adjusted Timeform ratings which the winners have achieved in the same race in the last five years. If the adjusted rating of the top-rated horse in a field made up mainly of lightly-raced horses is below the level of the TRW figures, the backer would be well advised to tread carefully. Timeform ratings have a considerable influence on the way the bookmakers bet, and it makes bad sense to take a short price about a horse whose weight-adjusted rating is below the TRW figures. There may well be something better among the unexposed.

In the following table, we have selected some of the most important flat races of the season for each age-group (the figure in brackets denotes their status, Group 1, 2 or 3), and listed the Timeform ratings achieved by the winners to the right of their previous best Timeform rating. (All figures are based on Timeform's end-of-season re-handicap).

Older Horses (4-y-o's +)

| | John Porter Stakes (3) | Sagaro Stakes (3) | Jockey Club Stakes (2) | Ormonde Stakes (3) |
|---|---|---|---|---|
| 1992 | 123-121 | 86-104 | 117-122 | 123-124 |
| 1991 | 116-113 | 114-113 | 116-113 | 115-111 |
| 1990 | 100-125 | 97-114 | 117-123 | 115-115 |
| 1989 | 131-125 | 95-110 | 131-122 | 125-115 |
| 1988 | 113-115 | 110-113 | 115-117 | 101-106 |

| | Yorkshire Cup (2) | Coronation Cup (1) | Hardwicke Stakes (2) | Ascot Gold Cup (1) |
|---|---|---|---|---|
| 1992 | 124-122 | 122-124 | 124-122 | 124-114 |
| 1991 | 110-115 | 127-123 | 124-121 | 115-111 |
| 1990 | 115-118 | 123-125 | 125-122 | 111-114 |
| 1989 | 125-116 | 123-125 | 129-125 | 122-115 |
| 1988 | 126-115 | 133-122 | 117-121 | 120-127 |

Older Horses (3-y-o's +)

| | King's Stand Stakes (2) | Princess of Wales's (2) | July Cup (1) | Eclipse (1) |
|---|---|---|---|---|
| 1992 | 125-120 | 124-126 | 119-121 | 123-125 |
| 1991 | 115-125 | 124-120 | 111-128 | 121-125 |
| 1990 | 114-137 | 118-117 | 107-122 | 118-121 |
| 1989 | 123-118 | 124-126 | 127-131 | 129-135 |
| 1988 | 119-120 | 117-131 | 128-128 | 134-134 |

| | King George & Qn Eliz (1) | Internat'l (1) | Qn Eliz (1) | Champion (1) |
|---|---|---|---|---|
| 1992 | 133-135 | 123-128 | 120-129 | 128-130 |
| 1991 | 139-138 | 121-124 | 125-129 | 119-125 |
| 1990 | 122-131 | 116-124 | 123-130 | 124-127 |
| 1989 | 135-135 | 124-128 | 133-137 | 124-128 |
| 1988 | 134-134 | 127-127 | 128-136 | 132-133 |

## Three-Year-Olds

| | 2,000 (1) | 1,000 (1) | Dante (2) | Derby (1) |
|---|---|---|---|---|
| 1992 | 120-119 | 110-117 | 117-117 | 119-127 |
| 1991 | 109-124 | 117-121 | 109-122 | 115-135 |
| 1990 | 118-127 | 121-122 | 108-117 | 108-127 |
| 1989 | 106-127 | 112-117 | 97-122 | 127-129 |
| 1988 | 124-124 | 121-121 | 113-125 | 110-130 |

| | Oaks (1) | St James's Palace (1) | King Edward (2) | St Leger (1) |
|---|---|---|---|---|
| 1992 | 108-128 | 117-121 | 106-116 | 128-122 |
| 1991 | 106-122 | 127-127 | 101-120 | 124-125 |
| 1990 | 122-127 | 112-122 | 98-116 | 125-130 |
| 1989 | 122-126 | 126-126 | 117-119 | 114-117 |
| 1988 | 120-126 | 103-127 | 122-113 | 121-130 |

## Two-Year-Olds

| | Coventry (3) | July (3) | Richmond (2) | Gimcrack (2) |
|---|---|---|---|---|
| 1992 | 85-99 | 98-105 | 87-107 | 92-107 |
| 1991 | 107-114 | 89-109 | 114-115 | 100-109 |
| 1990 | 101-105 | 78-110 | 105-106 | 118-118 |
| 1989 | 87-106 | 106-113 | 83-108 | 113-113 |
| 1988 | 97-114 | 88-103 | 98-102 | 97-108 |

| | Middle Pk (1) | Cheveley Park (1) | Dewhurst (1) | Racing Post (1) |
|---|---|---|---|---|
| 1992 | 109-118 | 96-116 | 117-126 | 101-132 |
| 1991 | 120-117 | 106-109 | 113-116 | 121-124 |
| 1990 | 115-116 | 98-113 | 110-115 | 103-120 |
| 1989 | 102-117 | 108-114 | 108-116 | 116-122 |
| 1988 | 113-113 | 105-116 | 115-128 | 106-123 |

## Average Figures

| | | Difference |
|---|---|---|
| 4-y-o's + | 117.48 (117.95) | 0.47 |
| 3-y-o's + | 123.75 (127.95) | 4.20 |
| 3-y-o's | 115.00 (123.25) | 8.25 |
| 2-y-o's | 103.13 (113.75) | 10.62 |

The first thing to be said about these 'average' figures is that they are not mathematically sound. We are not comparing like with like, and one age-group's Group 1 may be another age-group's Group 3. Nevertheless, the figures have value, even if they are not exactly illuminating. Not exactly illuminating, because everyone knows that a rating for a horse into its third or fourth season is much more likely to be near the mark than one for a first-season performer that might have raced only two or three times: of value, because they serve to illustrate just how wide the gap can be at times between the level of form achieved by a young inexperienced horse and the level of form it may be capable of achieving. Appreciation of this point is essential if the Timeform subscriber is to understand the ratings. We sometimes forget that all top-class performers have to start somewhere. And they don't start by showing top-class form in maiden and minor events. Some—for example, Sayyedati (116p), Mashaallah (123), Lahib (129) and Selkirk (129), to name four of Timeform's champions for 1992—were beaten on their first racecourse appearance. To regard these horses as having given an indication of their merit when they were beaten in these races would be ludicrous. So our advice to the reader would be to see Timeform ratings for all horses on the flat below the age of four not as measurements of merit but as assessments of form, whether the ratings carry a 'p' symbol (indicating likely improvement) or not. It is not for nothing that two-year-olds are referred to as juveniles; and even three-year-olds still have some growing up to do. See them as immature athletes who can improve from one race to the next, or show improved form from one race to the next, for any number of reasons. And be happy to leave the knowledge of exactly how good these 'babies' are to those who know no better.

With jump racing structured very much differently from its flat counterpart, it is impossible to provide a precise equivalent 'over the sticks'. However, by way of an illustration that the basic principles hold, we can consider the following examples provided by the non-handicap races run at the Cheltenham Festival:-

Novices & Juveniles

|      | Trafalgar Hse Hurdle | Arkle Chase | Sun Alliance Hurdle |
|------|------|------|------|
| 1993 | 143-150 | 125-152 | 124-134 |
| 1992 | 126-146 | 140-140 | 131-141 |
| 1991 | 116-147 | 147-153 | 145-145 |
| 1990 | 142-136 | 102-141 | 141-151 |
| 1989 | 123-152 | 129-148 | 139-146 |

Novices & Juveniles cont...

|  | Sun Alliance Chase | Daily Express Triumph Hdle |
|---|---|---|
| 1993 | 149-136 | 127-133 |
| 1992 | 145-152 | 114-148 |
| 1991 | 120-140 | 115-149 |
| 1990 | 138-145 | 123-137 |
| 1989 | 128-147 | 121-139 |

Others

|  | Champion Hurdle | Queen Mother Chase | BonusPrint Stayers' Hdle | Cheltenham Gold Cup |
|---|---|---|---|---|
| 1993 | 165-167 | 148-148 | 144-157 | 161-174 |
| 1992 | 130-164 | 167-172 | 168-162 | 164-170 |
| 1991 | 165-170 | 154-165 | 144-164 | 157-171 |
| 1990 | 163-167 | 174-164 | 150-159 | 148-168 |
| 1989 | 152-167 | 159-168 | 158-169 | 182-170 |

|  | Christies Foxhunter Ch | Cathcart Chase | National Hunt Chase |
|---|---|---|---|
| 1993 | 114-122 | 142-149 | 113-113 |
| 1992 | unraced-127 | 118-134 | 113-124 |
| 1991 | 107-134 | 143-143 | 108-116 |
| 1990 | 142-142 | 150-134 | no rating-116 |
| 1989 | 145-138 | 110-146 | 126-134 |

The average figures show a difference for novices and juveniles collectively of 14.20, while those for others is 7.91. Interestingly, the least difference (3.0) exists for the Queen Mother Champion Chase, a recognised championship event, usually contested by horses with proven ability at a high level; while the most (21.2) is for the Daily Express Triumph Hurdle, a race for juveniles, most of which by that stage have yet to be tested fully.

An understanding of the ratings leads to a better understanding of the thinking behind them, and towards a sharper eye for value. Here is an illustration. Two-year-old A wins a maiden race by two lengths and two-year-old B wins a Group 3 race by a similar margin. In the normal course of events it would be reasonable to conclude that B would be entitled to the higher form rating. But suppose B had run second in the race won by A and A had not been out since. That would be different, wouldn't it? Or would it? No, not at all. It is a strong probability, if not a racing certainty, that B has improved considerably. But not everyone is going to see it that way. And the backer may find excellent value betting against A on its next racecourse appearance.

The figures in our table are interesting and instructive, but of value only in those handful of races (the Cheveley Park Stakes, the 1,000 Guineas and the Oaks) where the runners are known to be meeting at level weights. For instance, we can see that a filly going into the Cheveley Park Stakes with a rating of 115 would have shown form good enough, in Timeform's opinion, to suggest (other things being equal) that she would have won three of the last five runnings of the race. The TRW figures, however, are of greater value, as they are weight and age based, enabling us instantly to judge how any horse stands in comparison with the winners of the same race in the last five years. A horse with a rating, age and weight adjusted, higher than that achieved by any of the last five winners would (again, all other things being equal) be an odds-on chance in anyone's book. Valuable information indeed!

The recent wholesale reconstruction of the Flat-racing programme to promote more competitive racing and to provide more opportunities for modest horses means that we are unable to publish TRW figures for as many races. The omission will rectify itself—one hopes—with the passing of time, but in the meanwhile the Timeform subscriber is in the dark as to the level of form required to win these newly-constructed races. And short of giving educated guesses, there is nothing we can do about it. Calculating figures for the few level-weight races the conditions for which have not been altered is complicated enough, and involves consideration of the age of the runners, the racecourse, prize money, the size of the field, and the time of the year when the race is run. For two-year-olds a five-runner maiden event at Newmarket in May normally takes more winning than a five-runner maiden event at Catterick in May, but less winning than a ten-runner maiden event at Newmarket in May and less winning than a five-runner maiden event at Newmarket in August. A two-year-old with a rating of 80 would normally be a 3/1-on chance to win a five-runner maiden at Catterick in May, an even-money chance to win a nine-runner maiden at Warwick in July, and around 12/1, probably, to win a twenty-runner maiden at Newmarket in the autumn. Speaking generally, with three-year-olds the longer the horse remains a maiden the worse it usually is: so from mid-season onwards we can expect the standard of runners competing in maidens to decline.

## Timeform Commentaries

'Other things being equal' is a convenient 'get-out' clause in case things don't work out. Which happens quite often. Races are won by the best horses *in the conditions* and not necessarily by the best horses at the weights. Which is another reason why Timeform top-rated horses get beaten. Identifying those horses which are unlikely, for one reason or another, to give their running is one of the functions of the *Timeform Commentaries*. With lightly-raced horses the commentaries are not of much help in this respect, but the importance of their role in underlining the *potential* of lightly-raced animals is considerable. This is an area where Timeform scores hands-down. Nowhere will the backer be provided with a better indication of the potential of an unraced or lightly-raced horse than through its Timeform comment. If the TRW figures indicate the top-rated to be vulnerable a study of the commentaries will frequently lead the backer to a stand-out bet to beat it.

As the picture builds up, so the emphasis in the commentaries swings away from what a horse is likely to be and towards the horse that it has shown itself to be; and as a rule once the racehorse reaches the age of four its merit and racing character may fairly be said to be established. Not only do we know (or think we know) how good it is, we also know (or think we know) what *type* of horse it is: whether it is a sprinter or whether it is a stayer; whether it is a firm-ground specialist or whether it is a mudlark; whether it is temperamental or whether it is phlegmatic; whether it is a suitable mount for an inexperienced apprentice or whether it requires strong handling; whether it is genuine and consistent or whether it is unreliable and inconsistent. Where known, these characteristics are recorded in the commentaries for the Timeform subscriber to consider, and quite often a study of the commentaries will reveal that the probable winner, or the value bet in the race, is not the Timeform top-rated at all, but one rated close up behind it, better suited by the distance, more at home on the going, or perhaps with a particularly enthusiastic write up.

Of the various factors (other than the relative merits of the runners at the weights) which have a bearing on the outcome of a race, the most important (aside, occasionally, from the effect of the draw) is the ground. This is particularly so where older horses (four-year-olds and upwards) are concerned. As a generalisation, it may safely be assumed that most horses upwards of four years will be racing over their right distance. But the number of horses equally effective on all types of racing surface is rather less than most. To many the ground makes a difference that is very material indeed, and a backer should consider backing a horse unraced or unproven on the prevailing going *only* when he feels the odds justify the risk.

## Timeform Computer Timefigures

Timeform Computer Timefigures are expressed on the same scale as the ratings (i.e. age and weight adjusted) and are directly comparable. A time-rating higher than the form rating implies either that the time evidence suggests the horse's form is better than the Timeform handicapper, in his wisdom, feels justified in assessing it at, or that the form rating has been reduced, most likely in the light of recent poor performances. To the backer, the significant point about the Timefigures is that, unlike the ratings, they usually have little influence on the betting market. On the negative side, they can draw the backer's attention to the fact that a rating for a lightly-raced horse may be based on the dubious evidence of a moderately-run or slowly-run race: it is always reassuring to see a form rating backed up by a timefigure. We should point out, though, that only a small proportion of races are run at a pace strong enough to produce representative timefigures, so it follows that in races involving inexperienced horses, the best timeratings will frequently be below the respective form rating.

## Timeform At The Races

For the racegoer readily to make best use of the Timeform information all he or she has to do is to purchase a Timeform Race Card. It is some time since we demonstrated putting a Timeform Race Card through its paces at one of our Charity Day meetings at York. As an indication of the confidence we had in the Timeform service we gave two months notice of our intention to do so in *Timeform News*. In 1993, Timeform had the pleasure, for the first time, of sponsoring a complete 8-race programme at Bath. Purchasers of Timeform Race Cards for the meeting through Timeform House in Halifax were granted half-price admission to the paddock enclosure and were invited to come along during the afternoon and meet members of the Timeform staff in the Lansdown Room and to ask them questions about the Timeform service. Over six hundred of them did so.

## Bath Racecourse

When courses were graded into Groups (from 1 to 4) on the basis of the prize money they offered, Bath was categorised as a Group 3 racecourse, on a par with Hamilton in Scotland, Beverley and Pontefract in the North of England, Leicester and Nottingham in the Midlands and Windsor in the South. Considering that the ground there frequently gets very firm in the summer, the size of the fields stands up well with competitive racing the norm, albeit at a low level. Bath is a left-handed, oval track, just over 1½m in extent, with a run-in of ½m: the track is generally galloping rather than sharp. Our Timeform Race Card tells us there is no advantage in the draw. The going was on the firm side. Here's how things went.

'Some trainers never learn. If he'd only look at Timeform he'd know I don't stay more than a mile.'

## 2.15 THE TIMEFORM DAY AT BATH       1m5y
## MEDIAN AUCTION MAIDEN STAKES
## (F)
£3,500 added    3yo

---

**1 BAULKING TOWERS** 3 b.g. Kala Shikari 125 – Carrula (Palm Track 122)          —
437   [1992 6m⁵ 7d 8.1s 7m :: 1993 8s Apr 12] big gelding: has a round action: well    8′Nb   6m
beaten in maidens and handicap. *M. MCCORMACK*
9-0   Drawn 2                                                      M. Perrett
*Light green, yellow epaulets, armlets and star on cap (Baulking Racing)*

**2 BOLTROSE** 3 b.c. Electric 126 – Garnette Rose 74 (Floribunda 136) [1992 8s    —
755   7.1s :: 1993 6f May 5] compact colt: brother to 6f/7f performer Surrey Racing and
half-brother to several winners: dam seemed to stay 1m: signs of ability in
maidens: 50/1 and ridden by 5-lb claimer, never-dangerous eleventh of 20 at
Salisbury on reappearance. *K. WHITE*
9-0   Drawn 4                                                      J. Williams
*Light blue and orange diamonds, light blue sleeves, light blue cap, orange star
(Mrs Elizabeth Hitchins)*

**3 DANNY BOY** 3 b. or br.c. Damister (USA) 123 – Irish Isle 67 (Realm 129)       **95**
436   [1992 6g 7m⁴ 7m⁴ :: 1993 10s Apr 12] sturdy colt: progressive maiden at 2 yrs,   99′Nm  7m
fourth of 10 in £8,850 event won by Barathea at Newmarket final start: in need of   89′Nm  7m
race, led 6f when tailed off on reappearance: should stay 1m: possibly unsuited by
soft ground. *R. HANNON*
9-0   Drawn 10                                                     Pat Eddery
*Dark green, red chevrons, dark green sleeves, red cap (Mr Ivan Twigden)*

**4 DICKINS** 3 b.c. Green Ruby (USA) 104 – Rosie Dickins 59 (Blue Cashmere 129)   —
709   [1992 6d³ 7v⁵ a7g :: 1993 7f 12.3d 10.3g May 3] sturdy, angular colt: little sign of  51′Le  6d
promise since debut: sprint bred. *R. HOLLINSHEAD*                                 15′Nc  7v
9-0   Drawn 12                                                     K. Darley
*Purple, green chevron and sleeves, yellow cap, purple star (Dickins Ltd)*

**5 MASTER BEVELED** 3 b.g. Beveled (USA) – Miss Anniversary §§                    —
755   (Tachypous 128) [1992 8m 8d 6f May 5] lengthy, unfurnished gelding
with scope: fourth foal: dam temperamental sprint maiden banned from racing as
3-y-o: has shown signs of a little ability in maidens at Leicester (edgy), Newbury
and Salisbury: twice slowly away. *A. P. JONES*
9-0   Drawn 1                                                      N. Adams
*Cerise, black, white hoop, black sleeves, white collar, cuffs and hoop on cerise
cap (Mr A. A. King)*

**6 MORAN BRIG** 3 ch.g. Bustino 136 – Aunt Judy (Great Nephew 126) [1992
NR] 10,500Y: fourth foal: half-brother to quite useful 1988 2-y-o 7f winner Island
Mead (by Pharly) and a winner in Malaysia by Rousillon: dam well-beaten
daughter of Juliette Marny. *I. A BALDING*
9-0   Drawn 6                                                      S. O'Gorman
*Red, dark green disc, dark green and red hooped cap (Mr G. M. Smart)*

**7 THE EXECUTOR** 3 ch.g. Vaigly Great 127 – Fee 111 (Mandamus 120) [1992   **83**
721   6g 7m⁶ 7g 8.1s³ 8d⁵ :: 1993 9g⁴ May 3] lengthy gelding: fair maiden: ran well     88′Cp  8s
behind American Swinger in handicap at Kempton on reappearance: will stay         81′Ke  9g
beyond 9f: acts on soft ground: tends to carry head awkwardly. *R. F. JOHNSON*    81′Ke  7m
*HOUGHTON*
9-0   Drawn 9                                                      T. Quinn
*Dark blue, yellow chevron hoops, yellow cap (Exors of the late Mrs J. de
Rothschild)*

**8 TWO LUMPS** 3 b.g. Nomination 125 – Tea-Pot 77 (Ragstone 128) [1992 8s⁴   **72**
6.9v] leggy gelding: half-brother to middle-distance winner One For The Pot (by   77′Ba  8s
Nicholas Bill) and winning hurdler Mr Dormouse (by Comedy Star): dam
out-and-out stayer: encouraging fourth in maiden at Bath last September: below
that form but not knocked about once held in similar event at Folkestone
following month. *I. A. BALDING*
9-0   Drawn 5                                                      R. Cochrane
*Royal blue, yellow braces, yellow cap (Mrs M. A. Rae Smith)*

**9 ALTA VICTORIA (IRE)** 3 b.f. Fairy King (USA) – Sunland Park (Baragoi **85 p**
715   115) [1992 6g :: 1993 8g⁶ May 3] smallish, angular filly: half-sister to several   80 Ke   8g
winners, including one-time fairly useful middle-distance performer Gulfland
(by Gulf Pearl): dam unraced: backed at long odds, over 5 lengths sixth of 16,
staying on never dangerous under tender handling, to Aneesati in maiden at
Kempton: takes good hold, but bred to prove suited by further than 1m: likely to
improve again. *R. CHARLTON*
8-9   Drawn 7                                    S. Raymont
*Dark blue, pink seams, striped sleeves, pink cap (Mrs James Baker)*

**10 MIGAVON** 3 b.f. Sharrood (USA) 124 – Migoletty 59 (Oats 126) [1992 NR ::   **87**
640   1993 7d⁶ 8.2d⁴ Apr 27] 900Y: leggy, angular filly: unimpressive mover: sixth foal:   75 No   8d
half-sister to 1992 1m seller winner Champenoise (by Forzando) and winning   40 Nb   7d
hurdler Jabrut (by Young Generation): dam, 1½m winner, is half-sister to useful
Linda's Fantasy: fair form in maidens at Newbury and Nottingham: will stay
beyond 1m. *W. G. M. TURNER*
8-9   Drawn 3                                    Paul Eddery
*Emerald green, brown sleeves, emerald green armlets (Mr Laurie Snook)*

**11 PRINCESS SHAWNEE** 3 b.f. Ilium 121 – Hachimitsu 39 (Vaigly Great 127)
[1992 NR] first foal: dam 7f and 8.3f winner. *MRS M. MCCOURT*
8-9   Drawn 13                                   A. Tucker (3)
*Pink, black stars, pink sleeves, black cap (Mrs B. Taylor)*

**12 STRATTON FLYER** 3 b.f. Mas Media – Empress Valley (Gay Fandango
(USA) 132) [1992 NR] 1,000Y: fourth foal: half-sister to 3 winners abroad,
including Persian Valley (by Persian Bold), at up to 9½f in Ireland: dam never
ran. *H. S. HOWE*
8-9   Drawn 11                                   T. Lang
*Emerald green and yellow diabolo, yellow sleeves, orange armlets, orange cap
(Mr W. C. Evans)*

**13 TREBLE LASS** 3 b.f. Damister (USA) 123 – Stock Hill Lass 87 (Air Trooper   —
115) [1992 6v] first reported foal: dam stayed 1m: soundly beaten in maiden at
Hamilton last November when trained by M. Johnston. *B. J. MEEHAN*
8-9   Drawn 8                                    A. Munro
*Black and orange check, black sleeves and cap (Mr E. J. S. Gadsden)*

STARTING PRICES: 9/4 Danny Boy, Alta Victoria, 9/2 The Executor, 8/1 Migavon, 12/1 Two Lumps, 14/1
Moran Brig, 25/1 Dickins, 33/1 Boltrose, Treble Lass, Princess Shawnee, 50/1 Baulking Towers, Master
Beveled, Stratton Flyer

No TRW figures. Danny Boy's rating is backed up by a
timefigure of 99. His comment tells us he showed progressive form
in three races at 2 yrs, and was tailed off, after leading 6f, over 10f
on soft going on his reappearance a month previously; he 'should
stay 1m', and we can see from his form figures that he has shown
his form on a firm surface. It is a pity that we are unable to publish
any TRW figures. Danny Boy's basic rating is 81 against an average
in the low to middle 70's, so he is a performer with above-average
form in a decidedly below-average contest. On top of which he is
trained by Richard Hannon and ridden by Pat Eddery. His
reappearance performance might appear to take some of the shine
off him. But we think not. Possibly the soft ground was against
him, quite probably he didn't stay. In any case he led 6f, so he
didn't run all that badly: when horses weaken on soft ground, they
are apt to do so rapidly. The race will have put him right. What of
the others? Migavon's comment does not read well: she's leggy,
angular, moves unimpressively, and cost only 900 guineas as a
yearling: both her races so far have been on a soft surface, and she
has the pedigree of one who 'will stay further' than 1m. So, too,
does Alta Victoria, a smallish, angular filly sixth in one of her two

races. It is difficult to see either of these having the pace for this contest. The Executor, who has raced six times, looks a more likely sort and 'ran well' in a 9f handicap on his reappearance. But this race looks tailor-made for Danny Boy, a 5/4-on chance in anyone's book. Incredibly, Danny Boy is 9/4 *against!* One could search for a month or more without finding a better value bet than this one.

*Danny Boy comes through strongly in the closing stages and is well on top at the finish, winning by 2½ lengths from The Executor, with Two Lumps 5 lengths away third.*

SECOND RACE                                    TRW 83 75 72 82 87 (Average 80)

---

2.45          THE E.B.F. TIMEFORM RACE CARD          5f11y
                    MAIDEN STAKES (D)
                      £4,500 added   2yo

---

1 **ALPINE SKIER (IRE)** 2 b.c. (Feb 20) Nordico (USA) – Heather Lil (Ballymore 123) IR 22,000F, 19,000Y: second foal: half-brother to 3-y-o Fortis Pavior (by Salt Dome): dam never ran. *R. HANNON*
   9-0  Drawn 11                                      K. Darley
   *Maroon, light blue sleeves, light blue cap, maroon diamond (Mr P. D. Savill)*

2 **ANOTHERONE TO NOTE** 2 ch.c. (Apr 4) Beveled (USA) – Dame Nellie 84 (Dominion 123) fourth live foal: dam lightly raced, won at 7f at 2 yrs. *M. P. MUGGERIDGE*
   9-0  Drawn 14                                      B. Rouse
   *Black, yellow cross belts, yellow sleeves, black armlets, red cap (Noteworthy Friends)*

3 **BANDAR PERAK** 2 b.c. (Mar 26) Aragon 118 – Noire Small (USA) (Elocutionist (USA)) third reported foal: brother to modest 7f/1¼m performer Lucky Noire: dam won 3 races in Italy and ran over hurdles here. *S. DOW*
   9-0  Drawn 10                                      C. Rutter
   *Red, white hoops, white sleeves, red seams, white cap (Mr P. Ang)*

4 **BITE THE BULLET** 2 ch.c. (May 22) Ballacashtal (CAN) – Longgoe 70    —
   (Lorenzaccio 130) [1993 5m] leggy, unfurnished colt: seventh foal: dam showed some ability at 2 yrs but little at 3 yrs: 33/1, went left stalls and always behind in 13-runner maiden at Lingfield. *D. R. LAING*
   9-0  Drawn 6                                      J. Quinn
   *Dark green, red chevron, red sleeves, dark green armlets, dark green and red quartered cap (Mr T. H. Couchman)*

5 **BLUE BOMBER** 2 b.c. (Apr 6) Tina's Pet 121 – Warm Wind 84 (Tumble Wind    **79 p**
692  (USA)) [1993 5m⁵ May 1] 9,000Y: close-coupled colt: fifth foal: half-brother to    68 Nm 5m
   3-y-o Warm Spell (by Northern State), 6f and 1m winner at 2 yrs, and 6f winner Courting Newmarket (by Final Straw): dam 7f to 1¼m winner, is half-sister to Shoot Clear, Sally Brown and Untold: 9/2, around 7 lengths fifth of 11, running fast almost 4f, to Gold Land in maiden at Newmarket: sure to improve. *R. HANNON*
   9-0  Drawn 1                                      Pat Eddery
   *Royal blue, white cross belts, hooped sleeves, white cap (Mr David Thompson)*

6 **DESERT LORE** 2 b.c. (Jan 31) Green Desert (USA) 127 – Chinese Justice (USA) (Diesis 133) first foal: dam Irish 2-y-o 6f winner. *LORD HUNTINGDON*
   9-0  Drawn 13                                      L. Piggott
   *Purple, gold braid, scarlet sleeves, black velvet cap, gold fringe (The Queen)*

7 **JACOB BOGDANI** 2 ch.c. (Mar 21) Night Shift (USA) – Green's Collection 65 (High Top 131) first foal: dam stayer. *P. F. I. COLE*
   9-0  Drawn 2                                      T. Quinn
   *White, red cap, white spots (Richard Green (Fine Paintings))*

8 **MONSIEUR PETONG** 2 b.c. (Jan 23) Petong 126 – Little Madam 66 (Habat 127) fifth foal: closely related to 1988 2-y-o 5f seller winner Alo' Niko (by Mansingh) and half-brother to 3-y-o Lady of Shadows (by Ballacashtal): dam won twice over 5f. *M. R. CHANNON*
9-0   Drawn 5                                      Paul Eddery
*White, royal blue cross of lorraine, red sleeves, red and white check cap (Mr E. J. Fenaroli)*

9 **NORTHERN STARLIGHT** 2 b.g. (Mar 24) Northern State (USA) 91 – **53 p**
586   Ganadora (Good Times (ITY)) [1993 5g Apr 24] small, sturdy gelding: fourth foal: half-brother to 3-y-o 7f winner Homemaker (by Homeboy) and 7f (at 2 yrs) and 5.8f winner Leigh Crofter (by Son of Shaka): dam unraced: 33/1 and backward, showed up well to halfway in 21-runner median auction maiden at Leicester: should improve. *P. G. MURPHY*
9-0   Drawn 7                                    N. Adams
*Emerald green, dark blue cross belts and sleeves (Mr K. A. Leadbeater)*

10 **SILVER BRIEF** 2 gr.g. (May 7) Sulaafah (USA) 119 – Briefing (Rusticaro (FR) 124) first foal: dam, showed little on flat (in Ireland) and over jumps, is granddaughter of 1000 Guineas winner Pourparler. *MRS J. C. DAWE*
9-0   Drawn 15                                  G. Bardwell
*Black, large yellow spots, black sleeves, yellow spots, yellow cap, black spots (Mr Terry Cooper)*

11 **SUN CHIEF (IRE)** 2 b.c. (Mar 7) Cyrano de Bergerac 120 – Stop The Cavalry    **– p**
586   (Relko 136) [1993 5g Apr 24] 23,000Y: smallish, sturdy colt: seventh foal: half-brother to 3-y-o Miss Bridge (by Common Ground) and winners abroad by Auction Ring and Try My Best: dam never ran: 16/1, very slowly into stride and always behind in 21-runner median auction maiden at Leicester: should do better. *B. W. HILLS*
9-0   Drawn 17                                  D. Holland
*Royal blue and grey stripes, black cap (Pharoahs Lodge Ltd)*

12 **COLNE VALLEY** 2 b.f. (Feb 16) Mazilier (USA) 107 – Mary Miller 71 (Sharpo    **63**
624   132) [1993 5s³ 5d⁵ Apr 26] 3,400Y: compact filly: first foal: dam stayed 7f, is    55 Wi   5d
daughter of 5f-winning half-sister to Forzando: beaten 6 lengths or so in maidens    55 Wa   5s
won by Carrie Kool at Warwick and Antonia's Folly at Windsor. *R. F. JOHNSON HOUGHTON*
8-9   Drawn 12                                    R. Hills
*Royal blue, red star, red sleeves, white armlets, red and royal blue quartered cap (Mr C. W. Sumner)*

13 **GIGGLESWICK GIRL** 2 b.f. (Mar 14) Full Extent (USA) 113 – Princess Lucianne (Stanford 121S) first foal: dam unraced. *M. R. CHANNON* *non-runner*
8-9   Drawn 4                                    A. Munro
*Royal blue and yellow (quartered), black sleeves and cap (Mr M. Bishop)*

14 **JULIA TONGA** 2 b. or br.f. (Apr 19) Petong 126 – Miranda Julia 73 (Julio Mariner 127) fourth foal: half-sister to 3-y-o Home Affair (by Petoski): dam 7f winner. *P. G. MURPHY*
8-9   Drawn 9                                    J. Williams
*Rose and white (quartered), yellow sleeves and cap (Mr D. L. C. Hodges)*

15 **REIGNING ROYAL** 2 ch.f. (May 17) Tina's Pet 121 – Regency Brighton    **–**
733   (Royal Palace 131) [1993 5g May 3] leggy filly: fourth reported foal: half-sister to 7f seller winner Royal Resort (by King of Spain): dam showed little on flat: 33/1, burly and green, soon tailed off in 11-runner maiden at Warwick. *R. J. HODGES*
8-9   Drawn 8                                    S. Drowne (7)
*Yellow, red braces, red cap (Mr D. A. Morris)*

16 **SHE'S SWEET** 2 b.f. (Mar 28) Full Extent (USA) 113 – Foligno (Crofter (USA) 124) first reported foal: dam won at 1½m in Ireland. *MRS J. C. DAWE*
8-9   Drawn 16                                  W. Newnes
*Yellow, royal blue seams on sleeves, royal blue cap (Jac Dawe Racing Club)*

17 **TITANIA'S DANCE (IRE)** 2 br.f. (Apr 14) Fairy King (USA) – Camden    **–**
593   Dancer (Camden Town 125) [1993 5g Apr 24] 12,000Y: rather lengthy filly: sixth foal: half-sister to 3-y-o Last Lake (by Kings Lake) and modest sprinter Resucada (by Red Sunset): dam Irish 9.5f winner: 9/2 and bit backward, driven along before halfway and never a factor in 11-runner maiden auction at Ripon. *M. BELL*
8-9   Drawn 3                                    M. Hills
*Red, dark blue hoop, dark blue cap (Miss Lucille Boden)*

STARTING PRICES: 11/10 Blue Bomber, 3/1 Desert Lore, 10/1 Jacob Bogdani, 14/1 Sun Chief, Titania's Dance, Monsieur Petong, 16/1 Colne Valley, Alpine Skier, 25/1 Northern Starlight, Bandar Perak, 33/1 Reigning Royal, Bite The Bullet, Julia Tonga, 50/1 Anotherone To Note, She's Sweet, Silver Brief

The only race on the card with TRW figures. We can see that Blue Bomber's rating (his timefigure is 11 lb lower) suggests he would have won two of the last five runnings of the race, assuming we are on the mark with our assessment of his one previous run, that is. Sixteen runners for today's race is decidedly above the average, and if one didn't know one would suspect that today's winner might be required to record a level of performance higher than that indicated by the TRW figures. Confirmation that Blue Bomber is no good thing is provided by the note in his comment that he was beaten around seven lengths (roughly 20 lb) in a maiden at Newmarket. Bath maidens take less winning than maidens at Newmarket, but not 20 lb less winning. So Blue Bomber is vulnerable. Nor is there anything in his comment to make one hot-foot it to the nearest bookmaker to get on at 11/10. Is there a 'stand-out' bet to beat him? Well, two newcomers do take the eye—Alpine Skier, a 19,000 guineas Nordico colt from the same stable as Blue Bomber and 16/1 in the betting, which tells one all one needs to know about that one; and Desert Lore, a colt by the high-class sprinter Green Desert out of a Diesis mare, Chinese Justice, a winning Irish 2-y-o at 6f. Desert Lore has shortened to 3/1 from 4/1, so is evidently fancied. With 10/1 bar the two, and half the field at 25/1 or more, this represents (for those not averse to backing newcomers) one of those excellent each-way opportunities to which we have already made reference. Course bookmakers are unlikely to display a willingness to lay Desert Lore each-way, but there's always the telephone, and keen-eyed backers at home should have no trouble getting 'on'.

*Desert Lore just gets the better of a good finish with Jacob Bogdani. Blue Bomber finishes seventh.*

---

THIRD RACE                                                          TRW − − − − −

---

3.15        THE TIMEFORM SILVER TANKARD        1¼m46y
                 MAIDEN STAKES (D) (D.I)
              £4,500 added   3yo +   TWFA 3 9-2

---

**1 ARCTIC LINE** 5 b.g. Green Ruby (USA) 104 – Sally Ann III (Port Corsair 98)
[1992 NR] non-thoroughbred gelding: half-brother to several winners, including useful sprinter Another Risk (by The Brianstan) and 1¼m to 2m winner Arctic Rascal (by Arctic Kanda): dam never ran: in rear in 2 NH Flat races last October. *J. M. BRADLEY*
    9-12   Drawn 2                                           N. Adams
    *Yellow, black star, black and yellow quartered cap (Mr E. A. Hayward)*

2 **CHAPEL OF BARRAS (IRE)** 4 b.g. Bob Back (USA) 124 – Gay Honey      –
802  (Busted 134) [1992 NR :: 1993 10g 11.7m⁶ May 8] big, workmanlike gelding: sixth    4 Ba  12m
reported foal: half-brother to 1990 2-y-o 5f winner Petropower (by Petorius) and a
winning Irish hurdler: dam never ran: won NH Flat race in February: well beaten
in maiden at Leicester in April and minor event at Bath in May. *P. J. HOBBS*
9-12   Drawn 3                                                    J. Williams
*Purple, emerald green sash, emerald green cap (Hawkridge Farmhouse Cheese
Limited)*

3 **COLWAY PRINCE (IRE)** 5 b.g. Prince Tenderfoot (USA) 126 – El Cerrito     –
(Tribal Chief 125) [1992 NR] workmanlike gelding: well beaten in maidens and
handicap at 3 yrs for A. Stringer: won 2 selling handicap hurdles in February, and
ran creditably in non-seller May 8. *A. P. JONES*
9-12   Drawn 12
*Cerise, black, white hoop, black sleeves, white collar, cuffs and hoop on cerise
cap (Mr A. A. King)*

4 **THE GORROCK** 4 b.g. Petoski 135 – Aquarula 88 (Dominion 123) [1992 13m    –
720  16.9d :: 1993 12g May 3] no worthwhile form for a long time: blinkered last 3
starts. *A. J. CHAMBERLAIN*
9-12   Drawn 14   (blinkers)
*Yellow, royal blue stars, sleeves and star on cap (Mr E. H. Lodge)*

5 **BIJOU FIRE (NZ)** 5 b.m. Noble Bijou (USA) – Firefly (NZ) (Fraxinus 106)     –
[1992 NR] New Zealand-bred mare: sister to Gem Fire, listed-placed in New
Zealand: dam won 9 races between 3 and 6 yrs, at 7f to 1½m: unplaced in 5 races
in Australia, in May, 1992, last time. *J. W. HILLS*
9-7   Drawn 15                                                    M. Hills
*Royal blue and white check, red sleeves and cap (The Racing Club Limited)*

6 **FLAKEY DOVE** 7 b.m. Oats 126 – Shadey Dove 81 (Deadly Nightshade 107)    **85**
546  [1992 13.3f :: 1993 14.1g⁴ Apr 19] angular mare: tends to be unimpressive in    55 No  14g
appearance: 7½ lengths fourth of 5 to 7/2-on shot Allegan in minor event at
Nottingham on only second run on flat: may well prove suited by further than
1¾m: smart hurdler (well below best on very soft ground), won latest start May 3.
*R. J. PRICE*
9-7   Drawn 7
*Red, yellow disc, quartered cap (Mr J. T. Price)*

7 **UNIFICATION (IRE)** 4 ch.f. Double Schwartz 128 – Hydro Princess     –
(Pitskelly 122) [1992 8m] workmanlike filly: second foal: dam, placed twice (over
5f) at 2 yrs and once (over 1m) at 3 yrs in Ireland, is half-sister to useful Irish
sprinter Pitmarie: 33/1 and bit backward, soon struggling and only modest late
headway in 15-runner minor event at Kempton last June: moved moderately to
post. *R. AKEHURST*
9-7   Drawn 4                                                    R. Perham
*Dark blue, emerald green hoop and sleeves, hooped cap (New House Farm Livery
Stables)*

8 **BAYRAK (USA)** 3 b.c. Bering 136 – Phydilla (FR) 126 (Lyphard (USA) 132)    **– p**
592  [1992 8.2s :: 1993 10g Apr 24] compact, good-bodied colt: closely related to
French 1¼m and 10.5f winner Cupid Sea (by Arctic Tern) and half-brother to
useful maiden Mysteries (by Seattle Slew) and winning hurdler Landed Gentry
(by Vaguely Noble): dam won from 6f to 1m, and is daughter of good broodmare
Godzilla: well beaten in maidens at Nottingham and Leicester, short of room on
several occasions and not given a hard time in latter: should do better. *A. C.
STEWART*
8-11   Drawn 10                                                    W. Carson
*Royal blue, white epaulets, striped cap (Mr Hamdan Al-Maktoum)*

9 **BEAUCHAMP HERO** 3 b.c. Midyan (USA) 124 – Buss 102 (Busted 134)    **70 p**
[1992 7m 7d⁴] half-brother to numerous winners, including 14.1f winner    66′ Li  7d
Beauchamp Grace (by Ardross), fairly useful miler Imperial Ace (by Derring-Do)
and stayer Beauchamp Cactus (by Niniski): dam game performer at up to 11f:
fourth of 20 in maiden at Lingfield last September, staying on very well: will
improve again, particularly over middle distances. *J. L. DUNLOP*
8-11   Drawn 5                                                    A. McGlone
*Orange, black hoop, white cap (Mr E. Penser)*

**10 BLACK DRAGON (IRE)** 3 ch.c. Ela-Mana-Mou 132 – Indian Lily 100   **95 ?**
(Indian King (USA) 128) [1992 7d$^2$ 7m] lengthy, useful-looking colt: rather   97'Yo  7d
unfurnished: second foal: dam 2-y-o 5f winner: ½-length second of 7 to Kusamba
in York minor event last September: disappointing favourite in Newmarket
maiden following month: will stay 1¼m. *B. W. HILLS*
   8-11 Drawn 9                        M. Roberts
   *Maroon, white sleeves, maroon cap, white star (Sheikh Mohammed)*

**11 CAPTAIN'S GUEST (IRE)** 3 b.c. Be My Guest (USA) 126 – Watership   **78 p**
763  (USA) (Foolish Pleasure (USA)) [1992 NR :: 1992 10f$^2$ May 6] tall colt with scope:   67 Br  7d
third foal: dam maiden half-sister to Grade 1 13f (Turf) Canadian International
Championship Stakes winner Great Nell: 13/2, bit backward and green, 2½
lengths second of 14 to Exhibit Air in maiden at Brighton, always in touch: sure to
improve and should win a maiden. *G. HARWOOD*
   8-11 Drawn 13                       R. Hills
   *Royal blue, white braces, hooped sleeves (Mr K. J. Buchanan)*

**12 PREROGATIVE** 3 ch.g. Dominion 123 – Nettle 106 (Kris 135) [1992 NR ::   **86 p**
719  1993 8d$^4$ 8g May 3] lengthy gelding: second foal: half-brother to 4-y-o Keen Wit   53 Nb  8d
(by Kenmare): dam, 6f and 7.3f winner at 2 yrs, appeared to stay 1½m: fair form in
maidens at Newbury (better effort) and Kempton (still in need of race): will stay
beyond 1m: sure to improve. *I. A. BALDING*
   8-11 Drawn 1                       L. Dettori
   *Purple, gold braid, scarlet sleeves, black velvet cap, gold fringe (The Queen)*

**13 RUNAWAY PETE (USA)** 3 b.c. Runaway Groom (USA) – Pete's Damas   **80 p**
304  (USA) (Cutlass (USA)) [1992 NR :: 1993 8m$^3$ Mar 30] $3,500F: small, sparely-   60 Le  8m
made colt: second foal: dam unraced: sire, high class at 1¼m at best, won Travers
Stakes: 10/1, 4¾ lengths third of 12 to Embankment in maiden at Leicester,
staying on well from mid-division: went down well: should stay 1¼m: will
improve. *P. F. I. COLE*
   8-11 Drawn 8                       T. Quinn
   *Yellow and orange hoops, orange cap (Mr Thomas T. S. Liang)*

**14 WHATONE BELL** 3 b.c. Presidium 124 – Betbellof 65 (Averof 123) [1992
NR] half-brother to 7f winner Rag Time Belle (by Raga Navarro), also successful
over jumps, and 6f winner Laurenbel (by Dublin Taxi): dam 2-y-o 5f winner. *M. P.
MUGGERIDGE*
   8-11 Drawn 6                       B. Rouse
   *Red, grey hoop, purple cap (Mr L. V. Wadge)*

**15 MISS MICHELLE** 3 ch.f. Jalmood (USA) 126 – Southern Dynasty 81 (Gunner    —
819  B 126) [1992 NR :: 1993 7d 7m May 8] workmanlike filly: third foal: half-sister to
9.7f and 1½m winner Snow Blizzard (by Petong): dam best at 4 yrs, when suited
by middle distances: burly, well beaten in newcomers race at Newbury
(wandered badly left, for E. Wheeler) and maiden at Lingfield. *S. MELLOR*
   8-6 Drawn 11                     D. Harrison (3)
   *Grey, maroon diamond and diamond on cap (Mr T. M. Bowser)*

STARTING PRICES: 100/30 Captain's Guest, Prerogative, 9/2 Black Dragon, 6/1 Runaway Pete, 8/1
Beauchamp Hero, 9/1 Bayrak, 10/1 Flakey Dove, 25/1 Bijou Fire, 33/1 Chapel of Barras, 50/1 Colway Prince,
Unification, Arctic Line, Miss Michelle, Whatone Bell, 100/1 The Gorrock

This race has attracted a field of lightly-raced horses and is
complicated by the fact that the rating for the top horse, Black
Dragon, carries a query. How does one calculate a fair price for a
horse who, on dead ground at York on its first outing, ran well
enough to suggest he could win this race easily, and on ground
similar to today's at Newmarket on his only other appearance
badly enough to suggest he could easily win nothing? Perhaps
something happened to him at Newmarket that we don't know
about. His opponents here seem a motley bunch. Prerogative is a
gelding: the comment tells us he ran a better race when fourth on
dead ground at Newbury on his debut than he did on good ground

at Kempton (out of the first six) on his second appearance: to some it may be flying in the face of logic to have a 'p' on his rating, but he has been backward. Flakey Dove is a 7-y-o mare by Oats: she has been in good form over hurdles, but her flat figure comes from a slowly-run race (timefigure 55) over 1¾m at Nottingham when she was fourth of five behind an easy 7/2-on winner: conditions today are likely to prove too sharp for her. Runaway Pete is the second foal of an unraced mare: on his one run he was beaten just under 5 lengths in a field of 12 maidens at Leicester: he doesn't look much, 'small and sparely-made' and cost only 3,500 dollars as a foal. Captain's Guest, on the other hand, is a 'tall colt with scope': he is the third foal of a well-related mare: on his one appearance he was a 'bit backward and green' when beaten only 2½ lengths in a field of 14 maidens at Brighton. Brighton, an undulating, sharp track, is not the most suitable course to introduce a young horse to the business of racing, and there is a good chance that Captain's Guest, noted as 'sure to improve and should win a maiden' will do much better here. Of the others, Beauchamp Hero is a well-bred type fourth of twenty at Lingfield on the second of two appearances as a 2-y-o; and Bayrak is an exceedingly well-bred colt (dam rated 126) well beaten in two starts. As a rule choicely-bred horses are not run down the back for the purpose of a handicap mark, so the probability is that Bayrak has shown his trainer as little at home as he has shown the racegoer on the racecourse. From the commentaries, one would confidently expect Captain's Guest to beat all bar, possibly, Black Dragon, and it looks odds on one of these two will win. The market finds Captain's Guest co-favourite at 100/30 (.231) with Prerogative, and Black Dragon on 9/2 (.182). So the odds against the pair add up approximately to 11/8 (.421).

*Captain's Guest and Black Dragon have the race to themselves in the last ¼m, Captain's Guest getting well on top close home to win by 2½ lengths as Black Dragon is eased.*

---

FOURTH RACE                                                     TRW – – – – –

| 3.45 | THE TIMEFORM SILVER TANKARD | 1¼m46y |
| | MAIDEN STAKES (D) (D.II) | |
| | £4,500 added   3yo +   TWFA 3 9-2 | |

---

**1 FIELDRIDGE**  4 ch.g. Rousillon (USA) 133 – Final Thought (Final Straw 127)    **93**
584   [1992 10d² 10f² 11.9g 10.2d² :: 1993 10g Apr 23] tall, lengthy gelding: fairly useful   81'Ke  10d
    maiden at 3 yrs for C. Nelson: well below form final start at 3 yrs, and on   72'Sb  10f
    reappearance in Sandown handicap: should stay beyond 1¼m: easily best effort   71'Ba  10d
    on firm going. *C. P. E. BROOKS*
    9-12   Drawn 10
    *Cerise, white cross belts, black cap, white star (Mrs W. Tulloch)*

2 **RONEO (USA)** 5 ch.g. Secretariat (USA) – Zaizafon (USA) 119 (The Minstrel
584   (CAN) 135) [1992 9.5g⁴ 9.5g :: 1993 10g Apr 24] tall gelding: first foal: half-brother
to 3-y-o Zafonic (by Gone West): dam 2-y-o 7f winner, best at 1m at 3 yrs:
ex-French gelding: trained by M. Zilber, signs of a little ability in French
Provinces in 1992: sold 5,600 gns Tattersalls Autumn (1992) Sales: tailed off in
maiden at Leicester in April. *MISS JACQUELINE S. DOYLE*
    9-12   Drawn 2                                     S. Curran (7)
    *Orange, dark blue chevrons, orange sleeves, dark blue armlets, hooped cap (Mr*
    *Tom Ford)*

3 **SANDRO** 4 b.g. Niniski (USA) 125 – Miller's Creek (USA) 62 (Star de Naskra   **57**
(USA)) [1992 12s 13.1m⁵ 16.2g 11.5m² 12m 12g⁴ 11.7d] leggy gelding:   63' Ba  13m
inconsistent maiden (mostly with J. Fanshawe) at 3 yrs: stays 13f: best efforts on   45' Sb  12g
top-of-the-ground: below form in blinkers last 2 starts: poor winning hurdler (last
autumn), well beaten Mar 2. *R. J. BAKER*
    9-12   Drawn 11  (blinkers)                            A. Munro
    *Beige, dark blue seams, striped sleeves, dark blue cap (Mrs Merrilyn Rowe)*

4 **CLASS ATTRACTION (USA)** 4 b.f. Northern Baby (CAN) 127 –
Chellingoua (USA) (Sharpen Up 127) [1992 NR] second foal: half-sister to winner
in USA Auggies Here (by Hilal), twice Grade 3 placed at 8.5f: dam lightly-raced
maiden in France, placed over 1m: sold out of M. Moubarak's stable 5,300 gns
Newmarket Autumn (1992) Sales: fourth of 15 at Hereford, probably better effort
in NH Flat races in May. *M. C. PIPE*
    9-7   Drawn 8                                     M. Perrett
    *Pink, black stars, black sleeves, pink stars, pink cap, black star (Rosebrand Ltd)*

5 **GESNERA** 5 br.m. Rusticaro (FR) 124 – Joie d'Or (FR) (Kashmir II 125) [1992   **43**
10.8m⁶ 14.6d· 14.6g⁵ 11.8g³ 12.1s⁴ 14.1d 12.1s 16s a12g a12g] lengthy mare: has a   46' Le  12g
roundish action: poor maiden handicapper: stays 14.6f: acts on soft ground: no   38' Cp  12s
improvement in a visor. *K. WHITE*
    9-7   Drawn 15                                  J. Williams
    *Navy blue, emerald green diamond and cap (Mr A. C. Hall)*

6 **BARON FERDINAND** 3 ch.c. Ferdinand (USA) – In Perpetuity 90 (Great   **95 p**
736   Nephew 126) [1992 7g³ 7s³ :: 1993 10.3m² May 4] strong, lengthy colt: fairly   91 Ch  10m
useful performance when neck second to Stoney Valley in 11-runner maiden at   80' Sb   7s
Chester, short of room over 2f out and finishing strongly: will stay beyond 10.3f:   76' Ke   7g
acts on good to firm and soft going: takes good hold, and wears crossed noseband:
will improve again, and sure to win a maiden at least. *R. CHARLTON*
    8-11   Drawn 1                                R. Cochrane
    *Dark blue, yellow chevron hoops, yellow cap (Exors of the late Mrs J. de*
    *Rothschild)*

7 **DIG IN THE RIBS (IRE)** 3 ch.g. Digamist (USA) 110 – First Contact 79   **63**
(Simbir 130) [1992 7f⁵ 8d⁶ 8v⁶] tall, useful-looking gelding: half-brother to 1986   59' Re   8d
2-y-o 5f seller winner Helens Contact (by Crofter), later a prolific winner in Italy:
dam stayed 1m: beaten around 2 lengths when fifth in moderately-run minor
event at Doncaster last September: never dangerous but not knocked about in
maidens: subsequently gelded: looks sort to do better. *R. HOLLINSHEAD*
    8-11   Drawn 12                                K. Darley
    *Maroon, light blue sleeves, light blue cap, maroon diamond (Mr P. D. Savill)*

8 **JONSALAN** 3 gr.g. Robellino (USA) 127 – Nelly Do Da 78 (Derring-Do 131)   **76**
[1992 5m⁴ 5g⁴ 7g⁶ 7g⁶ 8g²] leggy gelding: has scope: moderate mover: much   74' Wi  5m
improved effort when second in nursery at Warwick last August, beaten head by   58' Sa   5g
Express Mariecurie, starting slowly and driven along in rear 3f out: will be suited   56' Le   7g
by middle distances: trained at 2 yrs by W. Carter. *T. G. MILLS*
    8-11   Drawn 5                                 W. Newnes
    *Royal blue, white disc, white cap, royal blue star (Mr Alan E. Ward)*

9 **LEEWA (IRE)** 3 b.c. Caerleon (USA) 132 – Princess Nawaal (USA) 86 (Seattle
Slew (USA)) [1992 NR] second living foal: dam 8.5f and 9f winner. *MAJOR W. R.*
*HERN*
    8-11   Drawn 9                                   J. Reid
    *Yellow, black epaulets (Sheikh Ahmed Al Maktoum)*

10 **MOSHAAJIR (USA)** 3 b.c. Woodman (USA) 126 – Hidden Trail (USA)   **– p**
759   (Gleaming (USA)) [1992 NR :: 1993 10g$^6$ 12f May 5] $100,000F: rangy, good sort   51 Le   10g
with scope: ninth foal: half-brother to numerous winners in North America,
including 2 stakes winners by Shecky Greene and Full Pocket: dam unraced:
better effort in maidens when about 15 lengths eighth of 14 to Master Charlie at
Salisbury last time (moved poorly to post), tending to hang left before being eased
final 1½f: type to do better. *A. A. SCOTT*
    8-11  Drawn 14                                              B. Raymond
    *Royal blue, white chevron, light blue cap (Maktoum Al Maktoum)*

11 **RED WHIRLWIND** 3 b.c. Shadeed (USA) 135 – Red Red Rose (USA) 90   **–**
485   (Blushing Groom (FR) 131) [1992 7g :: 1993 7g Apr 15] tall colt: fourth foal: closely
related to Irish 1½m winner Green Glen (by Green Dancer): dam 1m winner: well
beaten in minor event at Kempton last August and maiden at Newmarket (still
green) in April. *M. R. STOUTE*
    8-11  Drawn 6                                               D. Holland
    *Maroon, white sleeves, maroon cap, white star (Sheikh Mohammed)*

12 **ROLLING WATERS** 3 b.c. Robellino (USA) 127 – Idle Waters 116 (Mill Reef
(USA) 141) [1992 NR] 50,000Y: half-brother to several winners, including very
useful stayers Shining Water (by Kalaglow) and Secret Waters (by Pharly): dam
smart 1½m to 14.6f winner. *B. J. MCMATH*
    8-11  Drawn 7                                               E. Johnson
    *Orange, purple cross belts, halved sleeves, white cap, black spots (Back Hill
    Bloodstock Ltd)*

13 **SPICE BOX (USA)** 3 ro.g. Spicy Story (USA) – Jemima Puddleduck (USA)
(Goose Creek 116) [1992 NR] second known foal: dam maiden. *I. A. BALDING*
    8-11  Drawn 4                                               L. Dettori
    *Black, gold cross and stripe on cap (Mr Paul Mellon)*

14 **TAKE A FLYER (IRE)** 3 b.c. Air Display (USA) 100 – Venus of Stretham 107
(Tower Walk 130) [1992 NR] IR 1,100F, IR 1,350Y: half-brother to a winner
abroad by Busted and to winning hurdler Qualitair Fighter (by Hard Fought): dam
won 10 races at up to 1¼m, 7 of them at 2 yrs. *R. J. HODGES*
    8-11  Drawn 13                                              S. Drowne (7)
    *Royal blue, white hooped sleeves (Mr Richard Morecombe)*

15 **ZAAHEYAH (USA)** 3 ch.f. Irish River (FR) 131 – Shoag (USA) (Affirmed   **–**
571   (USA)) [1992 NR :: 1993 8m$^4$ 8.5d$^6$ Apr 22] lengthy filly: fourth foal: half-sister to   45 Bv   8d
1991 2-y-o 7f winner Showgi (by Topsider) and a winner in Sweden by Northjet:   40 Le   8m
dam once-raced half-sister to Prix de Pomone winner Sweet Rhapsody and smart
American filly Sisterhood: better for race still, beaten over 15 lengths when sixth
of 16 to Chatoyant in maiden at Beverley: should stay beyond 8.5f. *J. R.
FANSHAWE*
    8-6  Drawn 3
    *Red, white hoops, striped sleeves and cap (Mr Mohamed Suhail)*

STARTING PRICES: 2/5 Baron Ferdinand, 8/1 Leewa, 10/1 Fieldridge, Spice Box, 16/1 Zaaheyah, 20/1 Red
Whirlwind, 25/1 Sandro, Jonsalan, 33/1 Class Attraction, Moshaajir, Dig In The Ribs, 50/1 Rolling Waters,
Take A Flyer, 66/1 Gesnera, Roneo

We can see from the comment that on his reappearance the
thrice-raced Baron Ferdinand, a 'strong, lengthy colt', was beaten
only a neck, finishing strongly, in an 11-runner maiden at Chester:
he 'will improve again and is sure to win a maiden at least'. The
4-y-o Fieldridge is close enough on the figures to suggest he is
capable of giving Baron Ferdinand a race. Fieldridge was trained by
C. Nelson at 3 years, but is now with C. Brooks, and was 'well
below form' in a handicap at Sandown on his reappearance: he
stays 1¼m and his best effort is on firm going. The others look too
far behind to merit serious consideration. Leewa and Rolling
Waters are newcomers bred well enough to suggest that they may
make racehorses one day, but there is no apparent confidence

behind them here. So it is a question of whether Baron Ferdinand to win at 2/5 is a better value bet than Fieldridge each-way at 10/1. We shouldn't think there is the slightest doubt about it. He isn't.

*Baron Ferdinand lands the odds comfortably, going ahead entering the last furlong. Fieldridge leads until the winner goes on. Leewa finishes a promising third.*

FIFTH RACE

---

4.15          THE TIMEFORM PERSPECTIVE &          1m5f22y
              RATINGS FILLIES HANDICAP (D)

£4,500 added   3yo+ fillies and mares   (Rated 0-80)   TWFA 4 9-12, 3 8-12

---

**1 SPECTACULAR DAWN**  4 gr.f. Spectacular Bid (USA) – Early Rising (USA)  **81**
432  (Grey Dawn II 132) [1992 8d 10g⁶ 10f* 10.2m 10m* 9.9d* 12d⁵ 13.1f² 11.7s³ ::  80'Ba  13f
1993 16s Apr 12] leggy filly: progressed well in handicaps in 1992, winning at  77'Ba  12s
Lingfield (twice) and Beverley: fit from hurdling but ran poorly in £8,000 event at  67'Fo  12d
Kempton on reappearance: stays 13.1f: probably acts on any going: usually raced
prominently in 1992. *J. L. DUNLOP*
9-12  Drawn 3                                          W. Carson
*Red and royal blue (quartered), white sleeves, black cap (Mr Peter S. Winfield)*

**2 TRUBEN (USA)**  4 ch.f. Arctic Tern (USA) 126 – Cadbury Hill (USA)  **86**
725  (Northern Baby (CAN) 127) [1992 12g* 12.3m* 12.5m² 12.3g⁴ 11.9d 12g⁴ 12g ::  83'Nm  12g
1993 13.8g⁴ 16.4g 12.4d² May 3] lengthy, sturdy filly: good mover: fairly useful  83'Wa  13m
handicapper: creditable efforts in frame at Catterick in March and Newcastle in  77'Fo  12g
May: stays 13.8f, not 16.4f: acts on good to firm and dead ground. *D. R. LODER*
9-11  Drawn 8                                          L. Dettori
*Black, white chevron hoop and cap (Lucayan Stud Limited)*

**3 ELAINE TULLY (IRE)**  5 b.m. Persian Bold 123 – Hanna Alta (FR) (Busted  **87**
134) [1992 12.5g⁴ 12g³ 8f² 11.9f⁵ 13.1g³ 14g] sturdy mare: fairly useful  94'Sb  12g
handicapper: better suited by 1½m/13f than shorter: acts on good to firm and  91'Ba  13g
dead ground: suitable mount for lady rider: well beaten in fair novice hurdle Mar  88'Yo  12f
27. *M. J. HEATON-ELLIS*
9-7  Drawn 2                                          J. Reid
*Yellow, emerald green diamond, emerald green diamonds on sleeves and cap
(Mr F. J. Sainsbury)*

**4 ATHAR (IRE)**  4 b.f. Master Willie 129 – Walladah (USA) 71 (Northern Dancer)  **83**
734  [1992 8d 12s⁵ 10f 10m 9.7h⁴ 8f 8f⁴ 12d 12.1s* 10.2s² 12s⁴ 10.2d :: 1993 10.8g²  80'Cp  12s
May 3] leggy, workmanlike filly: moderate mover: fair handicapper: fit from  77'Sb  12s
hurdling, good second of 17 to Here He Comes at Warwick on reappearance:  72'Fo  10h
effective at 1¼m to 1½m: acts on soft going, probably not on top-of-the-ground:
has won for an apprentice. *R. J. BAKER*
8-10  Drawn 6                                          A. Munro
*Dark green, white chevrons, halved sleeves, white cap (Mr J. W. Buxton)*

**5 JADIDH**  5 b.m. Touching Wood (USA) 127 – Petrol 73 (Troy 137) [1992 a12g ::  —
802  1993 11.7m⁵ May 8] leggy, plain mare: lightly raced and no worthwhile form on  35 Ba  12m
flat since 3 yrs: blinkered in 1992: modest form over hurdles in latest season. *MRS
J. C. DAWE*
8-3  Drawn 9                                          G. Bardwell
*Yellow, dark blue star, yellow sleeves, dark blue seams, dark blue cap (Mr Don
Hazzard)*

**6 CHILD STAR (FR)**  4 gr.f. Bellypha 130 – Miss Shirley (FR) 76 (Shirley  **83**
Heights 130) [1992 a10g² a10g a10g⁶ 14.6g² 12.3d 14.6g* 12.3m a14g⁵ 14.6g  85'Wa  16s
16.1s* 16s* a16g⁴] angular, light-framed filly: has a round action: modest  67'No  16s
handicapper: won at Wolverhampton last July then Warwick and Nottingham
last October: suited by a test of stamina: acts on soft going, below best on
all-weather surfaces. *D. MARKS*
8-1  Drawn 1                                          S. Dawson
*Yellow and emerald green hoops, emerald green sleeves, yellow armlets, green
diamonds on cap (Mr P. J. Pearson)*

**7 ATLANTIC WAY** 5 gr.m. Bold Owl 101 – Overseas 48 (Sea Hawk II 131) **85**

762 [1992 a14g a12g* 12d³ a12g³ 10s² 11.9g* 12d³ 11.9d 11.8d a12g a12g² a16g³ ::    78'Sb   10s
1993 a14g* a12g² a16g* a12g⁵ a12g⁶ a16g³ a12g* a14g⁵ 11.9s* 11.9g⁴ 11.9f May 6]   73'Br   12g
leggy mare: has a round action: modest handicapper: successful 3 times at   72 Br   12g
Southwell (in claimer third occasion) before winning at Brighton in April: well
below form at Brighton latest start: probably needs at least 1½m nowadays and
stays 2m well: acts on soft ground and fibresand, possibly not on firm going. *C. J.
HILL*

     7-10   Drawn 7                                    J. Quinn
     *Light blue, dark green and light blue striped sleeves, light blue and white
     quartered cap (Mr C. John Hill)*

**8 ROCQUAINE BAY** 6 b.m. Morston (FR) 125 – Queen's Royale 80 (Tobrouk **81**

762 (FR)) [1992 10.8d 12d⁴ 10m² 12f* 14s 11.9g² 12g² 12s :: 1993 11.9f³ May 6] leggy   86'Sb   12f
mare: poor handicapper: ran fairly well at Brighton on   72'Fo   12g
reappearance: better at 1½m than shorter, and should stay 1¾m: suited by a   72'Br   12g
sound surface nowadays. *M. J. BOLTON*

     7-7 (7-2)   Drawn 4
     *Emerald green, orange chevron (Mr D. C. Woollard)*

**9 RUBY DAVIES** 7 b.m. Ya Zaman (USA) – Tarpon Springs (Grey Sovereign    –
128§) [1992 NR] workmanlike mare: little worthwhile form in sellers and a
claimer in 1989 for J. Wilson: winning selling hurdler in 1989/90 for D. Burchell.
*D. J. WINTLE*

     7-7 (6-2)   Drawn 5                                    N. Carlisle
     *White, maroon triple diamond and sleeves, maroon cap, white star (Mr Gerald
     Hopkins)*

STARTING PRICES: 3/1 Truben, 7/2 Spectacular Dawn, 5/1 Athar, 11/2 Elaine Tully, 13/2 Rocquaine Bay, 7/1
Atlantic Way, 14/1 Child Star, 20/1 Jadidh, 66/1 Ruby Davies

Close on the ratings, but these races for older horses (there are
no three-year-olds in the field) often are. Elaine Tully is having her
first outing of the season, but the comment tells us she ran over
hurdles less than two months ago; she is 'better suited by 13f than
shorter' and 'acts on good to firm ground'; so everything is right for
her; what's more, she has three timefigures on the card all higher
than her form rating, which is most encouraging. Truben is also
suited by the distance and acts on the ground, and turned in
'creditable efforts' (roughly interpreted, within two or three pounds
of her rating) this season at Catterick and Newcastle. Atlantic Way
was very busy earlier in the year on the all-weather before winning
at Brighton; when 'well below form' at Brighton on her outing
previous to this one she was running on firm ground for the first
time in twenty-three starts this season and last. Child Star is
another making her seasonal reappearance: she is a winner over
2m on soft going and is 'suited by a test of stamina'. Athar, 'a good
second' (at the level of her rating) on her reappearance, has not
raced beyond 1½m and 'probably' does not act on top-of-the-
ground. Not exactly a two-horse race, but heading that way, with
Elaine Tully's edge over Truben offset possibly by the fact that she
is having her first race on the flat this season. In the circumstances
7/2 (.222) each of two, 5/4 (.444) the pair, would seem about right.
Truben is favourite at 3/1, with Elaine Tully at 11/2.

*Elaine Tully battles on gamely to come out best in a close finish
with Atlantic Way and Athar. It seems we were wide of the mark
when suggesting that the two last-named might not be suited by
firmish ground.*

# 4.45     THE JOCK JOHNSTONE TIMEFORM     5f11y
## LIMITED STAKES (F)
### £3,250 added   3yo   (Rated 0-65)

**1 AIR COMMAND (BAR)** 3 br.c. Concorde Hero (USA) 101 – Hubbardair 60   **71**
804   (Town And Country 124) [1992 5d³ 7.1g 6g³ 6d⁶ a6g⁶ a6g :: 1993 a5g⁴ a10g 8g   86'Sb   5d
5.1d* 5.7m May 8] close-coupled colt: modest form: trained reappearance by R.   76'Le   6d
Hannon, next start by S. Dow: won seller at Bath (sold out of J. Bridger's stable   65 Ba   5d
5,000 gns) in April: ran poorly in handicap at Bath 11 days later: stays 6f: acts on
dead ground: ran poorly in blinkers and eyeshield. *R. J. HODGES*
8-11   Drawn 9                                                T. Sprake
*Yellow, red star, armlets and star on cap (Mr Rhys Thomas Williams)*

**2 CREAGMHOR** 3 gr.g. Cragador 110 – Cawstons Prejudice 53 (Cawston's   **72**
629   Clown 113) [1992 5d³ 5s⁴ 5f⁴ :: 1993 5.1d Apr 27] rather leggy, close-coupled   78'Ri   5d
gelding: trained at 2 yrs by J. Berry when failed to progress from debut: off course   57'Re   5f
10 months, well below form in Bath seller: should be suited by 6f+. *M. J. BOLTON*   45'Hm   5s
8-11   Drawn 2                                                J. Williams
*Yellow, dark blue seams, armlets and cap (Mr A. R. M. Galbraith)*

**3 DISCO BOY** 3 b.c. Green Ruby (USA) 104 – Sweet And Shiny (Siliconn 121)   **66**
[1992 5d a6g⁵ 6d] poor form in autumn maidens at 2 yrs: stays 6f. *B. A.
MCMAHON*
8-11   Drawn 5                                                T. Quinn
*Red, black seams, black sleeves, red seams, red cap (Mr S. P. Bradford)*

**4 JEREMIAHS BOY** 3 gr.g. Sulaafah (USA) 119 – Main Chance 63   **71**
666   (Midsummer Night II 117) [1992 5.1d* 7m :: 1993 6g Apr 29] rangy, rather   78'Ba   5d
unfurnished gelding: poor mover: narrowly won maiden at Bath early at 2 yrs:
something clearly amiss when next seen out: off course nearly 9 months, very stiff
task but favourite, never able to challenge from rear after slow start when ninth of
14 in limited stakes at Salisbury on reappearance: bred to stay 1m+. *R. J.
HODGES*
8-11   Drawn 8                                                S. Drowne (7)
*Yellow, purple triple diamond, emerald green sleeves, yellow cap, purple
diamond (Mr J. Barber)*

**5 PURBECK CENTENARY** 3 b.c. Lidhame 109 – Double Stitch 74 (Wolver   **70**
630   Hollow 126) [1992 5g 5.1s 5g 6d 6s 5.1d :: 1993 a5g³ a6g² a6g² a6f² a7g* a5g³ 5.3g³   58 Br   5g
5.1d Apr 27] leggy colt: poor mover: best form on all-weather: claimed out of M.
Channon's stable £6,501 fourth start: won maiden at Lingfield in February:
creditable third at Brighton, below form at Bath 8 days later in April: stays 7f: best
form on good ground and on equitrack, yet to race on fibresand: has run
creditably for lady. *P. HOWLING*
8-11   Drawn 12                                               M. Roberts
*Beige and dark green diamonds, beige cap (The Hammond Partnership)*

**6 WINDRUSH BOY** 3 br.g. Dowsing (USA) 124 – Bridge Street Lady 93 (Decoy   **?**
323   Boy 129) [1992 5.1m² 5g² 5f 5m² 5.1m⁵ :: 1993 5g Mar 31] lengthy, leggy gelding:   90'Li   5g
fair maiden (rated 68) at 2 yrs: well below form last 2 starts, running as if   88'Fo   5m
something went amiss at Catterick in March: speedy: acts on firm ground. *M.*   88'Ba   5m
*MCCORMACK*
8-11   Drawn 1                                                J. Reid
*Royal blue, red star, red cap, royal blue star (Mr M. A. Wilkins)*

**7 CHAMPAGNE GRANDY** 3 ch.f. Vaigly Great 127 – Monstrosa 70   **86**
804   (Monsanto (FR) 121) [1992 5f 5d⁶ :: 1993 7m 6g* a7g 5.7m³ May 8] leggy,   83 Le   6g
close-coupled, sparely-made filly: has a quick action: modest performer: won   68 Ba   6m
seller at Leicester (bought in 6,500 gns) in April: good third, not given a hard time   67'Sb   5d
once held, to Hallorina in handicap at Bath on latest start: effective at around 6f
but should prove suited by further: acts on good to firm going, ran poorly on
fibresand. *M. R. CHANNON*
8-6   Drawn 10                                               Pat Eddery
*Beige and dark blue diamonds, beige sleeves, red cap (Grandy Girls)*

**8  CLOUDY REEF**  3 b.f. Cragador 110 – Kellys Reef 92 (Pitskelly 122) [1992 5m³  **79**
622  5f² 5.1g³ 5g⁴ 5.1m⁴ 5g³ 5m² 5f³ 5m³ 5g³ 5m⁶ :: 1993 5d⁵ a5g² Apr 26] small,   85′Ha  5g
good-quartered filly: poor mover: modest form at 2 yrs: below best in all-weather   83′Nc  5m
maiden at Southwell on latest start: yet to race beyond 5f but will be suited by   81′Th  5f
further: acts on firm going and probably on dead. *R. HOLLINSHEAD*
  8-6  Drawn 7                                                          K. Darley
  *Maroon, saxe blue sash, hooped cap (Mr M. Johnson)*

**9  HALLORINA**  3 b.f. Hallgate 127 – Diorina 91 (Manacle 123) [1992 5g 6f⁵ 5.1f  **88**
804  6m* 6.1g³ 6m* 6g 6.5m 5.2g :: 1993 5.7m* May 8] smallish filly: unimpressive   94′Go  6m
mover: improved form when winning 16-runner handicap at Bath in May by 1½   77 Ba  6m
lengths from Prince Songline: better suited by around 6f than 5f: acts on good to   73′Cp  6g
firm going, yet to race on a soft surface. *W. G. R. WIGHTMAN*
  8-6  Drawn 6                                                       G. Bardwell
  *Red, black cross belts and cuffs, lavender sleeves (Mrs J. A. Thomson)*

**10  LADY OF SHADOWS**  3 ch.f. Ballacashtal (CAN) – Little Madam 66 (Habat  **65**
629  127) [1992 6m 6g 5f⁶ 6m⁶ 5g 6m⁶ 6f³ 5.3f² 6m a6g a6g⁵ a8g a6g :: 1993 5.3g 5.1d   57′Sa  5f
Apr 27] strong, compact filly: poor maiden: burly, well beaten in 1993: stays 6f:   55′Ep  6f
acts on firm ground: has worn blinkers, visor and eyeshield: inconsistent. *S. DOW*   50′Br  5f
  8-6  Drawn 4  (visor)                                                 C. Rutter
  *Light blue, red chevrons and armlets, quartered cap (Under Orders Racing III)*

**11  MELODYS DAUGHTER**  3 b.f. Sizzling Melody 117 – Dancing Daughter 79  **82**
740  (Dance In Time (CAN)) [1992 5m 5d⁶ 5.7d⁶ 5d³ 5g* 5g⁵ :: 1993 6g 6.1m May 4]   81′Nm  5g
lengthy filly: unimpressive mover: modest performer: comfortably best effort   66′Ct  5d
when gamely making most to win Newmarket nursery last October: long way   56′Do  5g
below form in minor event at Brighton (no blinkers) and £7,300 handicap at
Chester (stiff task) this year: should stay 6f: blinkered last 3 starts at 2 yrs. *R. F.*
*JOHNSON HOUGHTON*
  8-6  Drawn 11                                                          R. Hills
  *Green and yellow hoops, yellow sleeves, quartered cap (Lord Leverhulme)*

**12  THE ORDINARY GIRL (IRE)**  3 b.f. Millfontaine 114 – Saulonika 94  **70**
754  (Saulingo 122) [1992 5g² 5.1s⁵ a6g³ a5g⁵ :: 1993 5f May 5] neat filly: has a round   69′Wo  5g
action: modest maiden: well below form on reappearance at Salisbury: stays 6f:   59′Ba  5s
acts on equitrack, below form on extremes of going: ran creditably in visor final
2-y-o start. *T. CASEY*
  8-6  Drawn 3                                                         N. Adams
  *Royal blue, red sash and diamond on cap (Mr M. Mac Carthy)*

STARTING PRICES: 2/1 Hallorina, 7/2 Champagne Grandy, 5/1 Windrush Boy, 9/1 Cloudy Reef, 12/1 Melodys Daughter, 20/1 Purbeck Centenary, 33/1 Air Command, Disco Boy, The Ordinary Girl, 50/1 Creagmhor, Lady of Shadows

This race has been named after Jock Johnstone, a Timeform customer for nearly 40 years. Only four in it on the ratings, and it is debatable whether the pluses and the minuses found in the commentaries narrow the gap between them or increase it. Cloudy Reef was 'below best' in an all-weather maiden at Southwell on the second of two outings this year, having raced eleven times in her first season. Melodys Daughter won a nursery last October; this year she has been 'long way below form' in her two starts: her best form is in blinkers and she is not wearing them. Hallorina and Champagne Grandy, on the other hand, are bang in form, and were first and third respectively in a 5.7f handicap on this course only nine days previously: the ground is no problem to either, but the distance (or rather the lack of it) is a worry; perhaps not so much here, as Hallorina and Champagne Grandy have a packet in hand on current form and we are talking about not much more than half a furlong; nevertheless, it would be foolish not to take account of the fact that neither has any form to speak of in its few attempts at 5f and Champagne Grandy 'should prove suited by further' than 6f; it cannot be to the advantage of either to be racing against a faster type of horse than that which it usually races against. Experience has taught us that in these situations it usually pays to err on the side of caution. Had there been no doubts about the effectiveness of Hallorina and Champagne Grandy at 5f, 2/1-on the pair would have seemed a fair price. It still seems a shade of odds on that one of the two will win, but whether Hallorina at 2/1 (.333) and Champagne Grandy at 7/2 (.222) add up to an attractive bet at 4/5 (.555) is open to question.

*Hallorina is well out of the race until coming with a 'rattle' inside the last furlong. Champagne Grandy also comes from behind. They finish respectively first and second.*

SEVENTH RACE

## 5.15 THE TIMEFORM RACEVIEW HANDICAP (E)   5f161y
### £4,000 added   4yo+   (Rated 0-70)

**1 BLUE TOPAZE** 5 ch.m. Fast Topaze (USA) 128 – Forever Mary 81 (Red Alert 127) [1992 5m³ 6g 6d* 5.7g* 7m³ 6g⁵ 7s 6m³ 6.1d³ :: 1993 6g* Apr 29] good-topped mare: fair handicapper: improved form on reappearance when trained by P. Murphy, decisively winning 14-runner event at Salisbury in April, staying on strongly from rear: effective at 6f, should prove at least as good over 7f: acts on good to firm and dead ground, seems unsuited by soft: suitable mount for lady rider. *M. S. SAUNDERS*
666
**75**
75' Ba  6g
70' Nm  6m
68 Sb  6g

    10-0  Drawn 14                        J. Williams
*Red and yellow (halved), sleeves reversed, yellow cap, red spots (Mr M. S. Saunders)*

**2 TRUTHFUL IMAGE** 4 b.f. Reesh 117 – Token of Truth (Record Token 128) [1992 6d⁵ 6d⁵ 5m* 5.7s 5m³ 6m⁴ 6m⁴ 5.7m* 5.7g 6g* 5g 6d 6m 5d⁵ 5.1d 5g a7g a6g⁵ :: 1993 6s⁶ 6g 6m May 8] good-topped filly: fairly useful handicapper: successful in 1992 at Windsor, Bath and Yarmouth: blinkered first time this season, badly hampered at start and did well to finish seventh at Lingfield last time: ideally suited by 6f: best on sound surface: blinkered or visored as 3-y-o: worth another chance. *M. J. RYAN*
815
**75**
73' Go  5d
70' Ya  6g
69' Wi  6m

    9-13  Drawn 6  (blinkers)             D. Biggs
*Red, black sleeves, white cap (Mr P. E. Axon)*

**3 CEE-EN-CEE** 9 b.g. Junius (USA) 124 – Lady Red Rose 87 (Pitskelly 122) [1992 a7g a6g⁵ 5.1d* 5.7m* 6m* 6g 5.7f² 7d 5.7g 5.1f⁴ 6g 5.7d⁵ 7d 5.1d :: 1993 5.1d 5.1m May 8] workmanlike gelding: has a round action: fair handicapper on his day: usually runs well at Bath, but missed break and always behind there on latest start: effective at 5f to 6f: acts on firm and dead ground: has won for apprentice: best in blinkers or visor though has won without: inconsistent. *MRS M. MCCOURT*
800
**73**
82' Ba  5f
78' Ke  6m
76' Ba  5d

    9-10  Drawn 7  (visor)             T. Quinn
*Royal blue, yellow chevrons and armlets (Mr D. N. Humphreys)*

**4 SAMSOLOM** 5 b.g. Absalom 128 – Norfolk Serenade 83 (Blakeney 126) [1992 5g 5m⁴ 5f⁶ 5m 6m 5.6m⁵ 5d 8m 5m³ 5m a6g³ a5g⁴ a6g⁴ a6g³ a6g⁵ :: 1993 a6g a6g³ a6g a7g* a7f a6g⁵ 6d* 6g Apr 24] strong, good-quartered gelding: has round action: modest handicapper: sold out of J. Balding's stable 3,200 gns Doncaster January Sales: won at Lingfield (claimer) in February and Brighton in April: fair ninth of 22 to Languedoc at Leicester on latest start: stays 6f, probably 7f: acts on any going, except soft: tried blinkered/visored once earlier in career: sometimes hangs left, and has found little: inconsistent. *P. HOWLING*
590
**70**
74' Re  5m
72' Do  5m
69 Br  6d

    9-9  Drawn 13                    J. Quinn
*Beige and dark green diamonds, beige cap (The Hammond Partnership)*

**5 CALL TO THE BAR (IRE)** 4 b.g. Kafu 120 – Papun (USA) (Mount Hagen **73**
630 (FR) 127) [1992 6g 6g³ 5.1g 6m 5g⁶ 5m⁴ 5g³ 5s* 5s :: 1993 5d³ 5.1d*ᵈⁱˢ Apr 27]   73 Ba  5d
leggy, sparely-made gelding: modest handicapper, trained at 3 yrs by C. Cox:  71' Wo  5s
better than ever in April, disqualified after winning gamely at Bath (edged left  68 Fo  5d
under pressure) last time: stays 6f: acts on soft going: below form when blinkered
(bolted) and visored once: has won for apprentice. *M. MCCORMACK*
    9-3   Drawn 2                         A. Clark
    *Purple and yellow diamonds, yellow sleeves, purple armlets, yellow cap (Trow*
    *Lane Farm)*

**6 ELTON LEDGER (IRE)** 4 b.g. Cyrano de Bergerac 120 – Princess of Nashua **69+**
677 (Crowned Prince (USA) 128) [1992 7s 7.6s 7m :: 1993 7d 6.1g⁶ 7g Apr 30]  45 No  6g
good-topped gelding: fair winning juvenile (rated 83) for J. Berry: best effort since
when sixth of 19 in handicap at Nottingham, keeping on: not discredited in face of
stiff task in 27-runner ladies handicap at Newmarket later in April: should prove
at least as effective at 7f as 6f: acts on good to firm ground. *A. A. SCOTT*
    9-3   Drawn 11                      B. Raymond
    *Black, white cross belts (Mr A. A. Scott)*

**7 COBBLERS HILL** 4 gr.g. Another Realm 118 – Morning Miss 59 (Golden **73**
630 Dipper 119) [1992 8m* 9.2m³ :: 1993 8f a6g 5.1d* Apr 27] plain, workmanlike  73 Ba  5d
gelding: best effort when promoted winner of 16-runner handicap at Bath in  59' Ay  8m
April, staying on strongly: effective at 5f and stays 1m: acts on good to firm and  12' Hm  9m
dead ground. *C. R. BARWELL*
    9-2   Drawn 1                        T. Lang
    *Pink and purple check, purple sleeves, pink cap (Miss S. Steel)*

**8 UNVEILED** 5 ch.m. Sayf El Arab (USA) 127 – Collegian 90 (Stanford 121§) **71**
668 [1992 5v 5d 7g 5.7m 5f⁴ 6m⁵ 7f 5.7g⁶ 5.7f³ 6g² 6g⁵ 5s 5.7d 6s 6.1d :: 1993 a7f a8g  71' Wi  6m
6d* 6.1g 6g Apr 29] sturdy, good-quartered mare: unimpressive mover: modest  71' Sb  5f
handicapper at best: has won one of last 25 starts, when straightforward task in  65' Sb  6g
Brighton claimer in April: below form since: ideally needs further than 5f, and
stays 7f: probably acts on any going on turf: inconsistent. *R. J. HODGES*
    9-2   Drawn 8                     W. Carson
    *Brown and orange (quartered), white cap (Mrs K. M. Burge)*

**9 RUSHANES** 6 ch.g. Millfontaine 114 – Saulonika 94 (Saulingo 122) [1992 a5g⁶ **72**
666 a6g⁵ a6g a6g² a5g⁴ a5g* a6g⁵ a6g³ a6g³ 5v* 5s⁴ a5g⁶ :: 1993 a6g a5g a6g a5g a5g⁶  72 Fo  5d
a7g⁴ a6g 6f⁵ 5d² 5s 6g⁶ Apr 29] small, sturdy gelding: poor mover: modest  66' Wa  5v
handicapper: stiff task, creditable sixth of 14 at Salisbury last time: effective at 5f  58 Sb  6g
and stays 7f: acts on any going and all-weather surfaces: ran poorly when
sweating and edgy: none too consistent. *T. CASEY*
    9-1   Drawn 12                      J. Reid
    *Royal blue, red sash and diamond on cap (Mr M. Mac Carthy)*

**10 DAWES OF NELSON** 8 b. or br.g. Krayyan 117 – Killyhevlin (Green God **71**
128) [1992 5g* 6m⁴ 5f 5s 6m³ 5m* 5m* 6g* 5d 6d] workmanlike gelding: has long  77' Hm  6g
stride: modest handicapper: at the top of his game last summer, landing hat-trick  67' Wi  5m
at Hamilton (2) and Windsor: effective at 5f, very best effort at 6f: acts on good to  66' Hm  5m
firm and soft going. *M. J. BOLTON*
    8-13   Drawn 4
    *Yellow, dark blue seams, armlets and cap (Mr A. R. M. Galbraith)*

**11 FARMER JOCK** 11 ch.h. Crofter (USA) 124 – Some Dame 72 (Will Somers **73**
114§) [1992 7m 6f 6f⁶ 6.1d⁴ 6g⁴ 6g² 7f⁴ 5.7f 6f⁵ 5g] strong, good-bodied horse:  81' Ya  6g
carries condition: only a modest handicapper these days: stays 6f: acts on any  68' No  6d
going: effective with or without blinkers or visor: tends to hang: is held up. *MRS*  63' Ya  6g
*N. MACAULEY*
    8-11   Drawn 15                  M. Roberts
    *Purple and royal blue (quartered), white sleeves, purple cap, white star (Mr S.*
    *Thompson)*

**12 GALLANT HOPE** 11 ch.g. Ahonoora 122 – Amiga Mia 71 (Be Friendly 130) **71**
815 [1992 6g⁵ 5.7m 6.1m² 5g⁶ 6d 6d³ 5f 5.1f³ 5.1m⁵ 6d 5.7d⁶ 6.1d :: 1993 6m May 8]  85' Ba  5f
small, stocky gelding: carries plenty of condition: has been hobdayed: only  77' Ep  5g
modest handicapper these days: last win came 54 starts ago, at 7 yrs: badly  63' Ba  6d
hampered at start on reappearance: suited by soft ground, acts on any other:
blinkered nowadays. *L. G. COTTRELL*
    8-11   Drawn 3                     N. Carlisle
    *White, red epaulets and armlets, red and yellow check cap (Mrs Nerys Dutfield)*

**13 TRIOMING** 7 b.g. Homing 130 – Third Generation 58 (Decoy Boy 129) [1992 **66**
449  6f 5m 7.6m 5d⁵ a5g³ 5.2g² 5g⁶ 6d :: 1993 5f* 5d 5s Apr 12] compact gelding:    69 Wa 5f
moderate mover: poor form: won maiden at Warwick in April: very stiff task in    62'Wo 5d
minor event next start, below form in handicap latest one: best at sprint distances:    60'Ya 5g
acts on firm ground and fibresand: below form when blinkered. *A. P. JONES*
    8-10  Drawn 5                                                   N. Adams
    *Cerise, black, white hoop, black sleeves, white collar, cuffs and hoop on cerise*
    *cap (Mr A. A. King)*

**14 SCARLET PRINCESS** 5 b.m. Daring March 116 – Noble Mistress 80 (Lord **74**
731  Gayle (USA) 124) [1992 7g 6g 6f 8.1m 6.1d* 6.1g³ 6f 7g 6.1g :: 1993 6g May 3]    79'No 6d
smallish, leggy mare: poor handicapper: form in 1992 only in July, winning at    78'Cp 6g
Nottingham: never dangerous in minor event on reappearance: stays 6.1f: suited
by give in the ground: inconsistent. *R. J. HODGES*
    8-2  Drawn 9                                              S. Drowne (7)
    *Beige and mauve diamonds, mauve sleeves, beige cap, mauve diamond (Mr D. J.*
    *F. Phillips)*

**15 GRAND TIME** 4 ch.c. Clantime 101 – Panay 77 (Arch Sculptor 123) [1992 **—**
362  a6g⁶ a5g* a6g² 5v 5.1d 5.7f 6g 5.7d 5m 5.1g a5g a5g :: 1993 a6g³ a5f⁵ a5g a6g Apr 5]
neat colt: modest performer: off the boil all but one of last 9 starts at 3 yrs:
creditable third in claimer at Southwell on reappearance but well below form
since, in a visor last time: stays 6f: possibly unsuited by heavy going: trained this
year by Mrs J. Dawe before rejoining 3-y-o trainer after latest start. *C. J. HILL*
    8-2  Drawn 10                                            G. Bardwell
    *Light blue, dark green and light blue striped sleeves, light blue and white*
    *quartered cap (Mr C. John Hill)*

STARTING PRICES: 9/2 Blue Topaze, 5/1 Truthful Image, 11/2 Call To The Bar, 6/1 Elton Ledger, 7/1 Cee-En-Cee, 12/1 Unveiled, Cobblers Hill, 14 Rushanes, 16/1 Farmer Jock, Scarlet Princess, 20/1 Dawes of Nelson, Gallant Hope, Samsolom, 25/1 Grand Time, 33/1 Trioming

When weighing up a race with a Timeform Race Card, one usually starts with the top-rated horse and works down. Well, the two top-rated horses in this race, Blue Topaze and the blinkered Truthful Image, are at the top of the card, so not only are they the best horses at the weights (in Timeform's opinion) they are the best horses in the race as well. It is the opinion of many that soft ground tends to magnify the effect of weight and to favour generally those at the bottom end of the handicap. So, under today's conditions, it is reasonable to suppose that the advantage, if any, will be the other way. Both Blue Topaze and Truthful Image have won over the course and distance, the former when the ground was good and the latter when the going was good to firm. We can see from the form figures that Truthful Image has also won over 5f on good to firm going (she is noted as 'best on a sound surface') whereas most of Blue Topaze's races, and all her other wins, have been over 6f. So not much doubt which is likely to be suited better by conditions today. In addition, the commentary on Truthful Image tells us she was 'badly hampered at start and did well to finish seventh' when blinkered for the first time this season on her latest appearance and is 'worth another chance'. Of those close to Blue Topaze and Truthful Image on the ratings, Scarlet Princess, who showed nothing on her only start this year, is 'suited by give in the ground'; Call To The Bar 'acts on soft going'; Cobblers Hill, a lightly-raced 4-y-o, put up 'best effort' on dead ground last time; Cee-En-Cee is a

9-y-o with no form in two races, once badly away, this season; and Farmer Jock is two years older than Cee-En-Cee and making his seasonal reappearance. It is difficult to ignore the claims of Truthful Image. 5/1 looks a backable price and unquestionably better value than 9/2 Blue Topaze.

*Truthful Image settles matters with a good turn of foot inside the final 2f and wins easing up. Blue Topaze, slowly away, does well to finish third.*

EIGHTH RACE

| 5.45 | THE TIMEFORM BLACK BOOK & RATINGS HANDICAP (E) | 1m5y |
|------|-----------------------------------------------|------|

£3,250 added   3yo+   (Rated 0-70)   TWFA 3 9-5

---

**1 SCOTTISH BAMBI** 5 ch.g. Scottish Reel 123 – Bambolona 108 (Bustino 136) [1992 7g⁴ 8g 10g* 10.8f* 10f⁵ 10m⁴ 10g* 10s⁵ 10m :: 1993 10m⁵ May 10] rangy, workmanlike gelding: has a round action: consistent handicapper: won at Leicester (gamely) last August: fair fifth of 13 to Akkazao in limited stakes at Windsor on reappearance, running as if race would put him spot on: will prove at least as effective at 1½m as shorter: acts on firm and dead ground: good mount for claimer. *R. HANNON*
843
**75**
79' Wa   11f
74' Wi   10g
70 Wi 10m

10-0   Drawn 13                                        D. Gibbs (7)
*Dark green, gold sleeves, scarlet cap (Mr William J. Kelly)*

---

**2 SILKY SIREN** 4 b.f. Formidable (USA) 125 – Smooth Siren (USA) (Sea Bird II 145) [1992 7d⁴ 8f⁶ 10g 8f⁵ 7g⁵ 10d 7g² 7m⁶ 6s :: 1993 a8g* a7g² 8f* 8g³ 7.6f³ May 6] sturdy filly: modest performer: won claimers at Southwell in February and Warwick in March: very good third in handicaps at Leicester and Chester (£7,400 event) since: stays 1m: acts on firm ground and fibresand: probably best in blinkers: races up with pace. *M. C. PIPE*
776
**75**
71 Ch   8f
59 Le   8g
57' Sb   8f

9-9   Drawn 4   (blinkers)                              Pat Eddery
*Emerald green, white epaulets, check cap (Mr S. Nixon)*

---

**3 LOCH DUICH** 7 ch.h. Kris 135 – Sleat 112 (Santa Claus 133) [1992 NR :: 1993 12g⁵ May 3] leggy horse: on flat since 5 yrs but fit from hurdling: fair form when fifth of 19 to Mr Geneaology in seller at Kempton in May: needs at least 1¼m and stays 1½m: acts on firm ground: has run well when sweating: takes keen hold. *R. J. HODGES*
720
**73**
66 Ke   12g

9-7   Drawn 10                                         S. Drowne (7)
*Red, white triple diamond, striped sleeves (Mr P. Slade)*

---

**4 BEATLE SONG** 5 b.m. Song 132 – Betyle (FR) (Hardicanute 130) [1992 a7g⁴ 6d 6v 6s 7m⁶ 5.7m 7.1m 7f⁴ 6m 7.1m* a7g 7g 7.1s :: 1993 a7g 6f 8g Apr 8] good-quartered, workmanlike mare: inconsistent handicapper: below form this season: trained until after latest start by R. Hodges: effective at 7f to 1m: acts on firm ground: sometimes pulls hard. *C. J. HILL*
413
**73**
65' Sb   7f
64' Cp   7m
57' Br   7m

9-5   Drawn 14                                         G. Bardwell
*Light blue, dark green and light blue striped sleeves, light blue and white quartered cap (Mr C. John Hill)*

---

**5 TOP ONE** 8 ch.g. Sallust 134 – Light Diamond (Florescence 120) [1992 a8g 8g 6g 8m* 8.2g a8g a7g :: 1993 a7g⁶ a8g⁴ a7g 6g* May 3] close-coupled gelding: form for a long time only when winning selling handicap at Yarmouth at 7 yrs and 19-runner minor event (led close home) at Warwick latest start: stays 1m: acts on any going: often bandaged: sometimes pulls hard. *C. J. HILL*
731
**67**
76' Ya   8m
48 Wa   6g

9-5   Drawn 1                                          J. Weaver (3)
*Light blue, dark green and light blue striped sleeves, light blue and white quartered cap (Mr C. John Hill)*

**6** **OCTOBER BREW (USA)** 3 ch.c. Seattle Dancer (USA) 119 – Princess Fager **71**
626 (USA) (Dr Fager) [1992 7f 7d 8m :: 1993 11.8g 8g⁵ 11.6d Apr 26] lengthy, 55 Br 8g
good-topped colt: fair maiden: creditable fifth of 17 to Woodwardia at Brighton in
April, easily best run this season: should stay beyond 1m: acts on good to firm
ground. *G. LEWIS*
9-3 Drawn 12 (blinkers) D. Harrison (3)
*Petunia, white hooped sleeves, pink cap (Mr David Barker)*

**7** **CREDIT SQUEEZE** 3 ch.c. Superlative 118 – Money Supply (Brigadier **69**
730 Gerard 144) [1992 5.2m 6g³ 5.1f 7m* 7m 7g 7d⁴ 6d :: 1993 8f³ 8g² 7g² May 3] leggy, 72'Ct 7m
good-topped colt: good mover: modest performer: in very good form in handicaps 67 Wa 7g
this season, staying on strongly behind Final Frontier at Warwick latest start: 67'Go 6g
effective at 7f and 1m: acts on firm and dead ground: consistent. *R. F. JOHNSON*
*HOUGHTON*
9-3 Drawn 7 R. Hills
*Lilac, primrose cross belts and sleeves, lilac cap (Mr R. C. Naylor)*

**8** **GOOD FOR THE ROSES** 7 b.g. Kampala 120 – Alleyn (Alcide 136) [1992 **74**
768 8.2m³ 8.2d 9g 8s* 8.2s² a8g⁴ a8g :: 1993 8g* May 6] leggy gelding: has a round 67'No 8m
action: modest performer: won 14-runner handicap at Carlisle on reappearance 65'No 8s
by 2½ lengths from Habeta: best form at 1m but may stay further: acts on any 63'Po 8s
going: should continue to give a good account of himself. *M. MCCORMACK*
9-0 Drawn 16 J. Reid
*Purple and yellow diamonds, yellow sleeves, purple armlets, yellow cap (Trow*
*Lane Farm)*

**9** **HEART OF SPAIN** 3 b.g. Aragon 118 – Hearten (Hittite Glory 125) [1992 6m⁶ **61**
286 5m⁴ a8g⁴ a8g² :: 1993 a8g⁶ a8g* 8f Mar 27] angular gelding: 8-length winner of 69'Go 6m
maiden at Lingfield, leading under 2f out: ran creditably facing stiffish task in 60'Sa 5m
Warwick handicap 3 weeks later: stays 1m: acts on firm ground and equitrack
(well below form on fibresand): yet to race on a soft surface. *P. J. MAKIN*
9-0 Drawn 16 B. Raymond
*Lilac, light blue cross belts, quartered cap (Mr J. S. Hobhouse)*

**10** **CHRISTIAN WARRIOR** 4 gr.g. Primo Dominie 121 – Rashah 67 (Blakeney **–**
126) [1992 7d 6d⁶ 7g 7.6s 7m⁴ 7.1m 6g 10g] neat gelding: no worthwhile form in 71'Go 7m
1992: blinkered (looked unenthusiastic) penultimate start: subsequently sold out 67'Ke 6d
of R. Hannon's stable 2,500 gns Doncaster August Sales. *R. E. PEACOCK*
8-12 Drawn 5
*Light blue, dark blue stripe, white cap (Miss P. Kissock-Smith)*

**11** **CHARMED KNAVE** 8 b.g. Enchantment 115 – Peerless Princess (Averof **75**
764 123) [1992 8m 7.1m² 8.1m⁴ 8f³ 7.1m² 8f 7g⁵ 7g 7.6g² 7g⁴ 7d 7s :: 1993 7f May 6] 78'Br 7m
lengthy gelding: poor mover: last win 16 starts ago, at 6 yrs: modest handicapper: 67'Ke 6d
well backed but below form on reappearance, soon pushed along but making late
headway not knocked about: effective at 7f to 1m: acts on firm and dead ground:
blinkered earlier in career. *D. R. LAING*
8-11 Drawn 8 T. Williams
*Light green, white braces, sleeves and cap (Mrs M. E. Olsson)*

**12** **ASTERIX** 5 ch.g. Prince Sabo 123 – Gentle Gael 97 (Celtic Ash) [1992 a6g⁵ 6d **73**
8.9g 9g 8.1m 7.1m³ 7d⁶ 7g 8f 7g] smallish, lengthy gelding: moderate mover: 66'Cp 7m
seems on the downgrade: effective at 6f to 1m: has form on any going: often 44'Wo 7d
visored. *J. M. BRADLEY*
8-11 Drawn 9 W. Newnes
*Black and light green check, pink sleeves and cap (Mr Clifton Hunt)*

**13** **PROUD BRIGADIER (IRE)** 5 b.g. Auction Ring (USA) 123 – Naughty One **73**
728 Gerard (Brigadier Gerard 144) [1992 a6g⁵ 7m 6.1m⁴ 6f³ 6.1g⁵ 6f² 6d 6m⁵ 6g² 6s² 80'Fo 6s
6.9v³ :: 1993 7g⁴ 8g⁴ May 3] lengthy, sparely-made gelding: poor mover: modest 73'Fo 6g
handicapper, trained at 4 yrs by W. Carter: creditable fourth of 21 in apprentice 44'Wo 7d
event at Warwick latest start: effective at 6f to 1m: probably acts on any turf going,
and equitrack: suitable mount for an apprentice: consistent. *M. R. CHANNON*
8-10 Drawn 11 T. Quinn
*White and black diabolo, white sleeves, royal blue armlets, royal blue cap (Mr M.*
*T. Lawrance)*

**14** **ROSIETOES (USA)** 5 b.m. Master Willie 129 – Desrose 74 (Godswalk (USA) **74**
728 130) [1992 8g 8.1m 7.1m⁶ 8.3m⁵ 10s 9g :: 1993 8g* May 3] leggy, angular mare: 67 Wa 8g
modest performer: 16/1, won 21-runner apprentice handicap at Warwick on 46'Wi 8m
reappearance, by 2½ lengths, leading over 1f out: stays 1m: acts on good to firm 45'Cp 7m
ground. *L. G. COTTRELL*
8-9 Drawn 18 Mark Denaro (7)
*Royal blue, emerald green braces and sleeves, emerald green and royal blue*
*quartered cap (Mrs Anne Yearley)*

**15  HOMEMAKER**  3 b.f. Homeboy 114 – Ganadora (Good Times (ITY)) [1992     **72**
662     5.1s² 6g 6m² 7f* 7m⁵ 5.7m⁴ 7d 7g² 8s :: 1993 7s* 7g⁵ Apr 29] workmanlike filly:     66'Br    7g
modest form: improved when winning handicap at Warwick in April: respectable     46'Wi    6m
fifth in similar event at Salisbury 16 days later: best form at 7f: probably acts on     59 Wa    7s
any going. *P. G. MURPHY*
8-8   Drawn 2                                                     J. Williams
*White, orange star, white sleeves, orange stars, white cap, orange star
(Racecourse Farm Racing)*

**16  RED SOMBRERO**  4 ch.g. Aragon 118 – Hat Hill (Roan Rocket 128) [1992 6g⁵     **72**
470     7d⁵ 8h 6g 7m³ 7f 8.3g² 7.1s⁴ 9d a8g :: 1993 6f 7s Apr 13] sturdy, close-coupled     69'Ep    7d
gelding: modest performer, still a maiden: well below form this season: stays 8.3f:     69'Sb    6g
acts on good to firm ground: well beaten in a visor fourth 3-y-o start. *R.*     66'Br    7m
*BROTHERTON*
8-5   Drawn 3                                                     A. Clark
*Light blue, dark blue seams, dark blue and yellow quartered cap (Mr J. R. Hall)*

**17  SAREEN EXPRESS (IRE)**  5 gr.g. Siberian Express (USA) 125 – Three     **73**
662     Waves (Cure The Blues (USA)) [1992 a6g a7g³ a8g⁴ a8g³ a10g⁴ a8g⁵ a7g6 a10g     79'Ba    8m
a8g* a7g⁴ a8g³ a8g⁵ 8.2m³ 8.1m⁶ 8m² 8.1g⁵ 8g 8.2m 7.1s³ 10g 8s 8s a8g* a8g⁶ a8g⁶     76'Cp    7s
:: 1993 a8g⁵ a8g³ a8g a8g a8g⁵ 8f 7g* Apr 29] lengthy, plain gelding: poor     70'Sa    8g
handicapper: won 20-runner apprentice race at Salisbury in April by short head
from Quick Steel, leading post: effective at 7f to 1m: acts on good to firm, soft
ground and on all-weather surfaces: often used to be blinkered, but not
nowadays. *MRS J. C. DAWE*
8-5   Drawn 6                                                     S. McCarthy (7)
*Yellow, dark blue star, yellow sleeves, dark blue seams, dark blue cap (Mr Don
Hazzard)*

**18  SARUM**  7 b.g. Tina's Pet 121 – Contessa (HUN) (Peleid 125) [1992 a7g² a8g³     **74**
818     a8g³ a8g* a8g* a8g* a7g² a7g³ 8m⁵ 8s a8g² 7m a8g⁵ a7g⁶ :: 1993 a8g a8g³ a8g³ a7g³     70'Br    8m
a7g³ a8g² a8g⁵ a7g⁶ a7g² a8g 7g a8g² May 8] tall, leggy, rather narrow gelding: poor
mover: modest handicapper: below form last 3 starts, beaten 7 lengths by Sylvan
Sabre at Lingfield last time: effective at 6f to 1m: acts particularly well on
equitrack, best form on turf on ground no softer than dead: has run well for
apprentice: genuine. *C. P. WILDMAN*
8-4   Drawn 17                                                    C. Rutter
*White, red sash and spots on cap (Mr W. Wildman)*

STARTING PRICES: 9/4 Silky Siren, 5/1 Good For The Roses, 9/1 Proud Brigadier, Credit Squeeze, 10/1
Homemaker, 12/1 Rosietoes, Scottish Bambi, 14/1 October Brew, 16/1 Charmed Knave, 20/1 Top One,
Sarum, Sareen Express, Beatle Song, Heart of Spain, 33/1 Loch Duich, Asterix, Red Sombrero, 66/1
Christian Warrior

Backing bad horses to win bad races is anathema to many and
we can get a good indication of the poor quality of runner in this
event from the fact that the 7-y-o Loch Duich, who carries third-top
weight of 9-7, gets his rating from running fifth of nineteen in a
seller over 1½m at Kempton. Scottish Bambi and Silky Siren are
the two set to carry more weight than Loch Duich, and what
applied to Blue Topaze and Truthful Image in the previous race
applies equally to Scottish Bambi and Silky Siren in this one,
except that they are joined on the ratings by Charmed Knave, an
8-y-o well beaten on its reappearance eleven days previously.
Scottish Bambi ran a 'fair' race on his reappearance, but his form is
at 1¼m and he 'will prove at least as effective at 1½m'. The
blinkered Silky Siren has already won twice at 1m this year and
acts on firm ground; she is the mount of Pat Eddery, but her price
of 9/4 in this field of eighteen is a 'joke'. It follows that if the
favourite is bad value there is a chance of good value elsewhere.
But where? Those not averse to backing apprentice-ridden light-

weights could do a lot worse than Sareen Express at 20/1: this one won a 20-runner apprentice race at Salisbury last time out and has a timefigure of 79 on the card recorded last year over today's course, ground and distance. Only Proud Brigadier, a 'consistent' 5-y-o, has a faster timefigure on the card than Sareen Express's. Proud Brigadier is interesting on two counts in addition to his timefigure; he was sent to be trained by Mick Channon at the start of the year, and until then had been campaigned over shorter distances. So what we are seeing with Proud Brigadier in this race is the reverse of the situation we encountered two races previously with Hallorina and Champagne Grandy: he has only to stay, which on breeding he is tolerably certain to do, for his speed to be seen to far greater effect against milers: we can see from his comment that Proud Brigadier has already been given a run at 1m this season, finishing a 'creditable fourth of 21 in apprentice event at Warwick'. Richard Quinn, one of the top jockeys in the country, has the ride on him this time, and Proud Brigadier, who acts on any going, is 9/1.

*Proud Brigadier has too much speed for these, and turns the race into a procession, idling in front before being eased near the line. Sareen Express finishes fourth, one place ahead of Silky Siren.*

'Perhaps he is a bit young but Timeform says he goes well for a boy.'

Well, the first thing we should say is not to be fooled by the results of one meeting. Every racing service has its good days. And if we are going to have a good day, we couldn't have picked a better one. Except perhaps the opening day of a major meeting. Because every racing service has its bad days, too. And if we are going to have a bad day, the opening day of a major meeting is scarcely the day for it. Just how wide of the mark the ratings, for example, were on the opening day of the big summer meeting at Goodwood two and a half months later may be judged from the fact that there was one second-top winner, at 5/1, and one top-rated placed in six races. The ratings picked up on the second day, with winners top at 10/1 (jt), 6/1 and 100/30, and another second-top at 4/1. Before detailing events on the third day, a few words about Goodwood racecourse.

## Goodwood Racecourse

Goodwood is a Group 1 racecourse. The five-day meeting there at the end of July represents one of the highlights of the racing year with quality of flat racing second only to Royal Ascot. One of the attractions of the big meetings is that clerks of the course seldom get the urge to alter races. So we are able to publish meaningful TRW figures. Goodwood is an undulating, right-handed track, essentially sharp in character, favouring the handy, fluent mover, rather than the big, long-striding horse. Our Timeform Race Card tells us that low numbers are favoured on the sprint course when the ground is soft. The going for the third day of the meeting was good to soft for the first four races, soft for the last three.

The Timeform Ratings and Commentaries, exactly as they appeared on the Timeform Race Card, and the starting prices for each race, are reproduced first without comment. This will enable the reader to put his own interpretation on the information before reading the way an experienced Timeform subscriber might have analysed the seven races.

## 2.30    THE LANSON CHAMPAGNE VINTAGE    7f
## STAKES (A) (Group 3)
£30,000 added   2yo

---

**1 BAL HARBOUR** 2 b.c. (Mar 2) Shirley Heights 130 – Balabina (USA) 110 **110 P**
2018 (Nijinsky (CAN) 138) [1993 7m* Jul 8] good-bodied colt: good walker: fluent 65 Nm 7m
mover: third foal: half-brother to French 3-y-o 1½m and 1¾m Palabac and 9f and
10.8f winner Balnibarbi (both by Rainbow Quest) and 1¼m winner, is sister to
good middle-distance performer Quiet Lady and Peacetime: heavily-backed
7/4-on shot though not fully wound up, won moderately-run 5-runner Child & Co
Superlative Stakes at Newmarket by a neck from Shepton Mallet, pair clear of
below-par Governor George, travelling well to dispute lead with runner-up over
1f out and running on well: sure to go on to better things. *H. R. A. CECIL*
9-0  Drawn 1                                                        Pat Eddery
*Green, pink sash and cap, white sleeves (Mr K. Abdulla)*

**2 BEAUTETE** 2 b.c. (Mar 1) Komaite (USA) – New Central 74 (Remainder Man **87 p**
1727 126§) [1993 6g* Jun 25] 1,000F, 3,300Y, 17,000 2-y-o: strong, good-quartered colt: 79 Go 6g
fourth foal: half-brother to 3-y-o Rosie's Gold (by Glint of Gold) and 1m winner
Jolizal (by Good Times): dam 6f to 1m winner: sire (by Nureyev) 7f winner
half-brother to Hours After and Belmont winner Avatar: 12/1, won 7-runner
maiden at Goodwood by a length from Bagshot, green and behind after slow start
then picking up really well from 2f out: will stay 7f: a promising debut, and is sure
to improve a good deal and win another race or two. *S. DOW*
8-11  Drawn 4                                                      L. Piggott
*Red, black cross of lorraine, white cap (Mr D. G. Churston)*

**3 CLASSIC SKY (IRE)** 2 b.c. (May 5) Jareer (USA) 115 – Nawadder 73 (Kris **110 p**
2242 135) [1993 6d³ 6f* 7m² 7g* Jul 17] good-topped colt: fourth foal: half-brother to 105 Yo 7m
2m winner Yaakum (by Glint of Gold): dam 7f winner, is out of half-sister to 100 Yo 6d
Bruni: much improved effort when beaten a neck by Bluegrass Prince in minor 78 Br 6f
event at York, looking all over winner when challenging on bridle but caught
close home: made hard work of simple task at Brighton over 6 weeks earlier but
didn't need to run to best when accounting for Cult Hero shade comfortably by ½
length in moderately-run 5-runner Mtoto Donnington Castle Stakes at Newbury:
much better suited by 7f than 6f: has a turn of foot: remains open to improvement.
*B. HANBURY*
8-11  Drawn 5                                                  W. R. Swinburn
*Royal blue, yellow chevron, yellow cap, royal blue spots (Mr Saeed Suhail)*

**4 LOMAS (IRE)** 2 b.c. (Mar 22) Ela-Mana-Mou 132 – Bold Miss (Bold Lad (IRE) **104 p**
1903 133) [1993 7g* 7.1m* Jul 2] 32,000Y: sturdy, rather angular colt: fifth foal: brother 102 Ke 7g
to modest middle-distance stayer Mystery Lad and half-brother to Irish 1¾m 80 Sa 7m
winner Tellyrand (by Cut Above): dam unraced: won 14-runner maiden at
Kempton in good style by 4 lengths (officially 6) from Silver Wedge: followed up
by 1½ lengths from Braille in 4-runner minor event at Sandown following month,
but wasn't impressive and needed to work hard after being held up in last place in
slowly-run race: will be better suited by 1m: likely to continue on the upgrade. *R.
HANNON*
8-11  Drawn 7                                                      A. Munro
*Dark green (Mr Fahd Salman)*

**5 MISTER BAILEYS** 2 b.c. (Feb 14) Robellino (USA) 127 – Thimblerigger 62 **101 p**
2242 (Sharpen Up 127) [1993 6m* 7g³ Jul 17] 10,000F, 10,500Y: sturdy colt: has plenty 98 Nc 6m
of scope: fine mover: half-brother to several winners here and abroad, including 70 Nb 7g
stayer Cleavers Gate (by Touching Wood): dam won at 1¼m: won 13-runner
maiden at Newcastle in really good style by 7 lengths from Level Sands: well
backed and looking very well, unlucky third to Classic Sky in moderately-run
5-runner £8,000 event at Newbury following month, running on well having been
short of room most of last 2½f: stays 7f: sure to win more races. *M. JOHNSTON*
8-11  Drawn 2                                                    Dean McKeown
*Yellow, dark green stripe, striped sleeves, quartered cap (G. R. Bailey Ltd (Baileys
Horse Feeds))*

**6 MR EUBANKS (USA)** 2 ch.c. (Mar 3) Imp Society (USA) – Whitesburg Lass **96** p
2018 (USA) (Whitesburg (USA)) [1993 7m* 7m⁴ Jul 8] 15,000Y: good-topped colt: has
scope: half-brother to 2 minor winners in North America: dam won at up to 9f:
quickened well when winning moderately-run 9-runner maiden at Newmarket
by 3½ lengths from Aljawab: looked very well when over 7 lengths fourth of 5 to
Bal Harbour in listed race there following month, staying on late having been
caught flat-footed over 2f out: may be capable of better. *P. A. KELLEWAY*
8-11 Drawn 6 J. Reid
*Light blue, purple epaulets, quartered cap (Roldvale Limited)*

77 Nm 7m
48 Nm 7m

**7 PRINCE BABAR** 2 b.g. (Mar 12) Fairy King (USA) – Bell Toll 87 (High Line **118**
2003 125) [1993 5d 5.2g* 6f² 6f³ Jul 7] 87,700 francs (approx £9,000) Y: sparely-made
gelding: has a round action: first foal: dam 2-y-o 7f and 1m winner: won 19-runner
median auction maiden at Newbury: has continued on the upgrade since in minor
event at Newbury (beaten easily by Lemon Souffle) and July Stakes at Newmarket
(outpaced early then came through to finish third to First Trump): may well be
even better suited at 7f: acts on firm ground (lost all chance at start on dead). *G. A.
PRITCHARD-GORDON*
8-11 Drawn 3 L. Dettori
*Cerise and white hoops, blue and white check cap (Mr Giles W. Pritchard-
Gordon)*

100 Nb 6f
97 Nm 6f
90 Nb 5g

STARTING PRICES: 13/8 Mister Baileys, 3/1 Lomas, 4/1 Prince Babar, 6/1 Classic Sky, 14/1 Beautete, 20/1 Mr
Eubanks

---

SECOND RACE (TV BBC1) TRW 123 128 116 125 121 (Average 123)

---

# 3.10 THE TIFFANY GOODWOOD CUP (A) (Group 3) 2m
### £40,000 added 3yo+ TWFA 4 9-12, 3 8-11

---

**1 ASSESSOR (IRE)** 4 b.c. Niniski (USA) 125 – Dingle Bay (Petingo 135) [1992 **126**
1536 10g³ 11.5s* 12g 11.9g³ 14.6m⁶ 15s³ 15.5s* :: 1993 12d⁴ 16.2g² 13.9d* 16.4g³ 20s²
Jun 17] useful-looking colt: fluent mover: smart performer: won Yorkshire Cup in
May by length from Allegan: ran very well when 3 lengths second of 10 to Drum
Taps in Gold Cup at Royal Ascot, pulling 6 lengths clear of remainder: effective at
1¾m to 2½m: best efforts on a soft surface: usually wears bandages: held up and
needs a truly-run race. *R. HANNON*
9-7 Drawn 6 T. Quinn
*Black, yellow cap (Mr B. E. Nielsen)*

114' Sa 10g
110 As 20s
99' Yo 12g

**2 ARCADIAN HEIGHTS** 5 b.g. Shirley Heights 130 – Miss Longchamp 94 **125** §
1536 (Northfields (USA)) [1992 12g⁴ 16.2d 13.4m² 16.4m² 20f² 16m⁴ :: 1993 16.4g⁵
20s⁵ Jun 17] lengthy, good-topped gelding: usually impresses in appearance: has a
fluent round action: very useful performer: twice bit opponent in 1992 and gelded
after going with little zest in net muzzle final start: off course 10 months, shaped
as if retaining his ability in steadily-run Henry II Stakes at Sandown: still carrying
plenty of condition, below form in Gold Cup at Royal Ascot 17 days later, staying
on past beaten horses for fifth, 20 lengths behind Drum Taps: stays 2½m: best
efforts on a sound surface and acts on firm ground: not one to trust. *G. WRAGG*
9-3 Drawn 1 L. Dettori
*Dark blue, white sleeves and cap (Mr J. L. C. Pearce)*

120' As 20f
114' Sa 16m
98 As 20s

**3 SONUS (IRE)** 4 b.c. Sadler's Wells (USA) 132 – Sound of Success (USA) **129**
2211 (Successor) [1992 10g* 12m⁴ 11.9g² 14.6m² 12m² :: 1993 11.8m* 12m³ 12d² Jul
16] good-topped colt: carries condition: very smart performer: runner-up in 1992
St Leger: narrow winner of listed event at Leicester in June: returned to his best
when 2 lengths second of 6, pair clear, to Always Friendly (rec 9 lb) in minor
event at Newmarket last time: effective at 1½m, at least when conditions are on
the soft side, and should stay 2m: acts on good to firm and dead ground: game. *J.
H. M. GOSDEN*
9-3 Drawn 7 (visor) Pat Eddery
*Maroon, white sleeves, maroon cap, white star (Sheikh Mohammed)*

121 Nm 12d
107' Nm 12m
107' Yo 12g

**4 DARU (USA)** 4 gr.c. Caro 133 – Frau Daruma (ARG) (Frari (ARG)) [1992 9.9g* **120+**
1536  10m⁶ 12m* 13.9g* 13.9g* 13.3s* 12g² :: 1993 12.3d* 13.9d 16.4g⁴ 20s Jun    115'Do  12g
17] close-coupled, workmanlike colt: good mover: very useful performer: won   109'Yo  14g
minor event at Ripon in April: very good fourth in steadily-run Henry II Stakes at   97'Yo  14g
Sandown in May: every chance on home turn but weakened quickly in straight in
Gold Cup at Ascot: may prove best at up to around 2m: acts on good to firm and
soft ground: wears a visor: tends to give trouble at stalls: found disappointingly
little under pressure third start: idles in front and is held up. *J. H. M. GOSDEN*
   9-0  Drawn 3  (visor)                                          R. Cochrane
   *Maroon, white sleeves, maroon cap, white star (Sheikh Mohammed)*

**5 JACK BUTTON (IRE)** 4 b.g. Kings Lake (USA) 133 – Tallantire (USA) **112**
1551  (Icecapade (USA)) [1992 12v* 12.3s⁴ 11.6m⁴ 12g 16.2d* 11.9f 16.2d* 18.5d² 16f*   103 As  20d
16.2d³ 16.2s* 16m⁶ 18m 16.5g² :: 1993 18f³ 16.2d* 16g³ 16.2g* 18.5m² 20d³    98'Ha  16s
22.2d² Jun 18] good-topped gelding: unimpressive mover: a useful performer:    90'Do  17g
won minor events at Haydock (unbeaten in 5 starts there) in April and May: has
run well in Chester Cup, Ascot Stakes and steadily-run Queen Alexandra Stakes
(short-headed by Riszard) since: suited by a test of stamina: probably acts on any
going: unsuccessful when tried in blinkers/visor on 4 occasions, but has run
creditably: very tough, game, genuine and consistent. *BOB JONES*
   9-0  Drawn 2                                                   N. Day
   *White, royal blue hoops, chevrons on sleeves (A. and B. Racing)*

**6 NOT IN DOUBT (USA)** 4 b.c. Tom Rolfe – Trillionaire (USA) 111 (Vaguely **121 ?**
1772  Noble 140) [1992 10d⁶ 12.1m* 14f* 14f³ 13.3d⁴ 14.6f 16m⁵ 14m² :: 1993 14g³   109'Nm 14m
16.2g⁴ 16.4g² 16.1m⁴ Jun 26] close-coupled colt: useful performer: improved form  101'Sb  14f
when in frame in steadily-run Sagaro Stakes at Ascot and Henry II Stakes at     100'Nm 16m
Sandown: appeared well handicapped on that form off his old mark in
Northumberland Plate but was off bridle before halfway and stayed on only
steadily for fourth behind runaway winner Highflying: stays 2m: best form on a
sound surface: ran creditably when blinkered last 2 starts in 1992, hasn't worn
them this year. *H. CANDY*
   9-0  Drawn 5                                                   J. Reid
   *Mauve and white check, striped sleeves (Mrs David Blackburn)*

**7 ANNE BONNY** 4 b.f. Ajdal (USA) 130 – Sally Browne 120 (Posse (USA) 130) **120**
1930  [1992 8g* 10g³ 10f² 10g 9d² 10g* 12g³ :: 1993 12g⁶ 10d2 11.9g⁵ Jul 3] big, lengthy  110'Sa  10g
filly: has a round action: useful performer: good efforts in minor event (behind   107'As  12g
Young Senor) at Newbury and Lancashire Oaks at Haydock last 2 starts: effective   107'Nm  10f
at 1¼m to 1½m: acts on firm and dead ground. *J. R. FANSHAWE*
   8-11  Drawn 4                                                  W. R. Swinburn
   *Royal blue, white cross belts, hooped sleeves, white cap (Mr David Thompson)*

**8 DI GIACOMO** 3 ch.c. Bustino 136 – Dark Amber 68 (Formidable (USA) 125) **109**
2100  [1992 NR :: 1993 10.5d* 12m* 14.5s² Jul 11] 5,700F, 5,400Y: third foal: dam, 1m
winner at 4 yrs, is half-sister to smart middle-distance stayer Rakaposhi King:
won 6-runner £11,200 events at Rome in May and Milan in June: ½-length
second of 4 in St Leger Italiano at Turin: stays 14.5f: fairly useful at the least. *J. L.
DUNLOP*
   7-12  Drawn 8                                                  W. Carson
   *White, pink spots, royal blue sleeves, pink cap (Mr G. Mazza)*

**9 MAGICAL RETREAT (USA)** 3 b.f. Sir Ivor 125 – Known Charter 96 **122**
2019  (Known Fact (USA) 135) [1992 7g 6v³ :: 1993 10s* 10g⁶ 10g* 11.4m³ 10g 12s⁶   117 Nm 15m
14.8m³ Jul 8] small, workmanlike filly: won maiden at Kempton and listed race   89 Ke  10s
(set slow early pace) at Newmarket in April: excellent third of 8 to Spring To    88 As  12s
Action in listed race at Newmarket latest start: may be better at 1¾m than shorter:
acts on good to firm and soft ground. *C. A. CYZER*
   7-12  Drawn 9                                                  D. Biggs
   *Yellow, black disc, black and yellow check cap (Mr R. M. Cyzer)*

STARTING PRICES: 6/4 Assessor, 4/1 Sonus, 9/1 Di Giacomo, 10/1 Magical Retreat, 14/1 Arcadian Heights,
Not In Doubt, Jack Button, Daru, 25/1 Anne Bonny

## 3.45 THE SCHWEPPES GOLDEN MILE (HANDICAP) (B) 1m

£65,000 added   3yo+   TWFA 3 9-8

---

**1 PETER DAVIES (USA)** 5 ch.h. Bering 136 – French Flick (USA) (Silent **111+**
1938  Screen (USA)) [1992 10s 12d :: 1993 7d² 8.5g* 8.1m* Jul 3] lengthy horse: won  108 Sa  8m
Racing Post Trophy at Doncaster at 2 yrs but had only 4 races over next 2 seasons  85 Ep  9g
and suffered hairline leg fracture in 1992: very useful performer nowadays: won  66 Yo  7d
minor event at Epsom in June and £12,800 handicap at Sandown in July: came
with steady run to lead inside final 1f and beat Talent by 2 lengths going away at
Sandown: effective at 1m and should be suited by around 1¼m: acts on good to
firm ground and soft: capable of better. *D. R. LODER*
     9-13  Drawn 10                                              L. Dettori
     *Black, white chevron hoop and cap (Lucayan Stud)*

**2 PAY HOMAGE** 5 ch.g. Primo Dominie 121 – Embraceable Slew (USA) **113**
2070  (Seattle Slew (USA)) [1992 8d 8g⁴ 8.1m* 8.9f³ 8f 8.1s⁵ 8g⁴ 9m³ 8.9m 8m 8g⁴ ::  104' Sa  8m
1993 a8g⁴ 8g³ 8d 8g* 8.1g* 7.6g Jul 10] angular, workmanlike gelding: very  99 Sa  8g
useful performer: won Jubilee Handicap at Kempton, rated stakes handicap at  99 Ke  8g
Beverley and Kingfisher Lager Whitsun Cup at Sandown (second year running,
best effort to beat Marastani by 2 lengths) all in May: never going pace over sharp
7.6f at Lingfield 6 weeks later, and last of 9 in rated stakes handicap: stays 9f: best
efforts on a sound surface, and acts on equitrack: blinkered once at 2 yrs, ran
creditably when visored final start at 4 yrs: has won for apprentice, not this year:
sometimes hangs right: held up and has turn of foot: game and genuine. *I. A.
BALDING*
     9-10  Drawn 9                                              M. Hills
     *Yellow, black hoop, white sleeves, black armlets (Miss A. V. Hill)*

**3 ABBEY'S GAL** 3 b.f. Effisio 120 – Outward's Gal (Ashmore (FR) 125) [1992 **112**
2470  6m³ 6g² 6m² 5d* 7.3g⁴ :: 1993 7g* 7.5d* 7.6m* 7g² 7s³ 7d³ Jul 27] lengthy filly:  100 Bv  7d
has a round action: successful in handicaps at Brighton, Beverley and Chester in  93 Nm  7g
the spring: placed in listed race (getting poor run) at Newmarket, Jersey Stakes at  89 Br  7g
Royal Ascot and listed event at Goodwood (most unlucky, persistently denied a
run in straight, eventually switched and quickening well, but still about ½ length
adrift of Moon Over Miami at line) since: suited by 7f to around 1m: acts on good
to firm and soft ground: bandaged behind: has good turn of foot and is held up:
flashes tail under pressure but is genuine: sweating latest start: remains in top
form. *I. A. BALDING*
     9-1  Drawn 1                                              W. R. Swinburn
     *Royal blue, yellow stripe, yellow sleeves, blue cap, yellow stripe (Mr Jerrard
     Williamson)*

**4 CUMBRIAN CHALLENGE (IRE)** 4 ch.g. Be My Native (USA) 122 – **115**
1474  Sixpenny (English Prince 129) [1992 10.1f³ 8.9d⁶ 8m² 8.9m⁴ 8m* 8m 9g* 9d ::  107' Nc  8m
1993 8.5m² 10g³ 8.9d⁴ Jun 12] leggy gelding: has a markedly round action: useful  104' Yo  9m
handicapper: ran very well in rated stakes handicap at Beverley (made most) and  101 Re  10g
Zetland Gold Cup at Redcar (raced prominently, 4 lengths behind River North)
first 2 starts this year: shaped as if still in good form at York on latest, steadied
stalls and not knocked about: stays 1¼m: acts on firm and dead ground: takes
good hold. *M. H. EASTERBY*
     9-1  Drawn 5                                              S. Maloney (3)
     *Royal blue, yellow star, white sleeves, royal blue cap, yellow star (Cumbrian
     Industrials Ltd)*

**5 LOST SOLDIER (USA)** 3 b.c. Danzig (USA) – Lady Winborne (USA) **113**
2253  (Secretariat (USA)) [1992 6f* 6g* 8s³ 7m :: 1993 7g⁶ 6.1d⁵ 8m⁴ 8d² Jul 17] rangy  102' As  8s
colt: has a round action: useful form: back to form last 2 starts, second of 7 to  96 Nm  8d
Beauchamp Hero in rated stakes handicap at Newmarket latest start: better at 1m  94' Nm  6g
than shorter: acts on any going: bandaged off-fore third start. *L. M. CUMANI*
     8-11  Drawn 12                                              R. Cochrane
     *Maroon, white sleeves, maroon cap, white star (Sheikh Mohammed)*

**6 PHILIDOR** 4 b.c. Forzando 122 – Philgwyn 66 (Milford 119) [1992 6g 8f* 8m **119**
1905 8m 8m* 7.9m⁴ 8s :: 1993 10.4d 10g² 8s³ 10m⁴ Jul 2] smallish, strong colt: fairly 120'Nb 8f
useful handicapper: in frame in Zetland Gold Cup at Redcar, Royal Hunt Cup at 117 Sa 10m
Royal Ascot and Royal Hong Kong Jockey Club Trophy at Sandown (looked in 105 Re 10g
magnificent shape, good fourth to Smarginato) last 3 starts: effective at 1m and
stays 1¼m: probably acts on any going: held up: has never been better. *J. M. P.
EUSTACE*
    8-7 Drawn 13                     N. Kennedy (3)
    *Purple, light blue chevron, light blue cap (Mr J. C. Smith)*

**7 STONEY VALLEY** 3 b.c. Caerleon (USA) 132 – Startino 111 (Bustino 136) **107**
871 [1992 NR :: 1993 7g⁴ 10.3m* 10.4d⁴ May 13] 56,000Y: rangy, angular colt: has a 103 Ch 10m
quick action: second living foal: half-brother to a 1992 German 1m winner by Be 88 Nm 7g
My Guest: dam 1m and 1½m winner also third in Park Hill: quite useful form 77 Yo 10d
when winning maiden at Chester in May: second favourite, well-beaten last of 4
to Commander In Chief in minor event at York 9 days later, weakening quickly
last 2f: will stay beyond 10.3f: acts on good to firm going. *P. W. CHAPPLE-HYAM*
    8-6 Drawn 20                     J. Reid
    *Emerald green, royal blue sleeves, white cap, emerald green spots (Mr R. E.
Sangster)*

**8 SHOW FAITH (IRE)** 3 ch.c. Exhibitioner 111 – Keep The Faith 86 (Furry **114**
1905 Glen 121) [1992 6m⁴ 5g³ 6d⁵ 7.3s² :: 1993 10m² 8g* 8d* 10m Jul 2] good-topped 100'Nb 7s
colt: led final 1f to win maiden at Newmarket in May and Britannia Handicap 96 As 8d
(favourite and looking tremendously well, still in rear 3f out when winning by 93 Wi 10m
length from Just You Dare) at Royal Ascot in June: very progressive to that point,
but never going well when second favourite in £46,000 handicap at Sandown
latest start: best efforts at 1m, but probably effective at 1¼m: very best effort on a
soft surface, though shaped well on good to firm on reappearance: useful. *R.
HANNON*
    8-5 Drawn 6                   Pat Eddery
    *Royal blue, grey sleeves, royal blue armlets, royal blue cap, grey star (Mr I. A. N.
Wight)*

**9 FOREVER DIAMONDS** 6 ch.g. Good Times (ITY) – Mel Mira 68 (Roi Soleil **115**
2056 125) [1992 8d* 8m⁵ 8.3s² 8m² 8.9g* 8s² 10m² 7.9s* 8s :: 1993 8d⁴ 8g⁴ 8g* 7v² 8.1s⁵ 113 Yo 8m
8.1d² 8s 7.9m* Jul 9] leggy, rather sparely-made gelding: fairly useful 107 Th 8g
handicapper: won £12,300 event at Thirsk in May and £7,500 contest at York 101'Yo 8s
(stayed on well under pressure to beat Buzzards Bellbuoy ½ length) in July:
effective at 7f, but ideally suited by further and stays 1¼m: acts on any going:
twice below form in blinkers: good mount for apprentice: tough, game and
consistent. *M. H. EASTERBY*
    8-5 Drawn 16                   M. Birch
    *Yellow, royal blue diamond, royal blue and yellow hooped sleeves, yellow cap,
royal blue diamond (Mrs J. B. Russell)*

**10 FROGMARCH (USA)** 3 ch.c. Diesis 133 – La Francaise (USA) (Jim French **113**
2365 (USA)) [1992 8v :: 1993 10m⁴ 7.9d* 8m⁵ 10g Jul 23] quite attractive colt: quite 87 Yo 8d
useful form: made virtually all to win 4-runner maiden at York in June: creditable 81 Nb 8m
efforts in minor event at Newbury and handicap at Ascot (edgy, kept on well from 73 Sa 10m
rear, not knocked about behind Moscow Sea) since: stays 1¼m: acts on good to
firm and dead ground. *MAJOR W. R. HERN*
    8-3 Drawn 3                   R. Hills
    *Brown, eton blue epaulets and cap (Lord Chelsea)*

**11 SHAMAM (USA)** 3 ch.c. Shadeed (USA) 135 – Goodbye Shelley (FR) 116 **116**
2020 (Home Guard (USA) 129) [1992 6s³ 7m² 7d⁴ 7.3g* 7g⁴ :: 1993 7g² 8g* 7.9d 8.5m³ 105 Ep 9m
8m² Jul 8] quite good-topped colt: fluent mover: won handicap at Newmarket in 101 Nm 8m
April: has continued in fine form, looking in superb shape before excellent 98'As 7g
second of 17 to Beauchamp Hero in £10,300 handicap at Newmarket latest start:
better suited by 1m than 7f and may stay 1¼m: acts on good to firm and soft
ground: consistent. *P. T. WALWYN*
    8-0 Drawn 8                   W. Carson
    *Royal blue, white epaulets, striped cap (Mr Hamdan Al-Maktoum)*

**12 PRENONAMOSS** 5 b.g. Precocious 126 – Nonabella 82 (Nonoalco (USA) **112**
2088 131) [1992 5.2d⁶ 6f³ 6f 7d⁵ a7g 7.1m 6g⁴ 7.1s⁴ 6d⁶ 7m⁴ 7d² 7g :: 1993 7f 7m⁴ 7m⁶ 117'Yo 7d
Jul 10] lengthy, rather angular gelding: quite useful handicapper: fair sixth of 11 108'Ay 6d
to Dune River at York on latest start: effective at 6f and 7f: acts on firm and dead 107'Nm 7m
ground: below form when blinkered: often bandaged: held up: consistent though
has won only 2 of 29 starts lifetime. *D. W. P. ARBUTHNOT*
    8-0 Drawn 7                   F. Norton
    *Black, yellow disc, diabolo on sleeves, quartered cap (Mrs W. A. Oram)*

**13 NORFOLK HERO** 3 b.c. Elegant Air 119 – Caviar Blini 80 (What A Guest **109**
1550    119) [1992 6m³ 6s* :: 1993 10.4d³ 10g 7f⁴ 8d Jun 18] leggy, quite attractive colt:    102 Nb   7f
fairly useful form: best efforts in frame in 4-runner minor event at York and rated   92 Yo   10d
stakes handicap at Newbury: not discredited in mid-division in Britannia   86'Nb   6s
Handicap at Royal Ascot latest outing, never able to challenge: may well ideally
need further than 1m: acts on any going: bandaged last 2 starts: pulled hard this
season. *D. J. G. MURRAY-SMITH*
    7-13   Drawn 19                   A. Munro
    *White and light green stripes, red sleeves and cap (Lady D. M. Watts)*

**14 DOUBLE FLUTTER** 4 b.f. Beldale Flutter (USA) 130 – Perfect Double 43 **109**
2396    (Double Form 130) [1992 9s³ 10f* 10g⁴ 9d³ 10.1g⁶ :: 1993 a10g³ 8m 8g⁴ 8.5m³   120'Nc   10g
10.1g 8s⁴ 10m 8g⁵ 8d Jul 24] lengthy, unfurnished filly: unimpressive mover:   96 Nb   8g
fairly useful performer, rated 92 at 3 yrs: not so good this season: ran creditably   95'Sb   10g
staying on over Ascot's straight mile in Royal Hunt Cup at Royal Ascot and, after 2
fair efforts, in £11,900 handicap behind Dawning Street last time: probably needs
testing conditions at 1m these days and should stay beyond 1¼m: acts on any
going, though well below form on equitrack: usually held up. *M. R. CHANNON*
    7-13   Drawn 4                   C. Rutter
    *Emerald green, red sash, emerald green sleeves, red seams, emerald green cap,*
    *red star (Mr John W. Mitchell)*

**15 NORTHERN BIRD** 3 ch.f. Interrex (CAN) – Partridge Brook 109 (Birdbrook **110**
1978    110) [1992 5g⁴ 5g* 6f³ 5.7m* 6m⁴ 6s 6d⁴ 6v :: 1993 6g⁵ 7d⁶ 7g* 7f Jul 6]   115'Nm   6d
close-coupled filly: fairly useful handicapper: led over 1f out to win at Epsom in   103'Yo   6m
June: ran creditably in mid-division in slowly-run rated stakes at Newmarket 5   99'Nm   5g
weeks later: stays 7f: acts on firm and dead ground (twice well beaten on very
soft): bandaged behind first and latest 3-y-o starts: game and consistent. *B. W.
HILLS*
    7-12   Drawn 11                  D. Biggs
    *Royal blue, emerald green cross belts, emerald green and royal blue quartered*
    *cap (Mr John E. Bradley)*

**16 BLOCKADE (USA)** 4 b.g. Imperial Falcon (CAN) – Stolen Date (USA) **116**
2250    (Sadair) [1992 8.2d³ 10m⁵ 10m* 9m³ 8g* 8f³ 8g* 8f* 7.9m⁶ 8g 8d :: 1993 7g 8.5g   118'Nm   8f
8m² 8f⁴ 8d² Jul 17] leggy, close-coupled gelding: tubed: quite useful handicapper:   114'Ba   8g
very good second of 10 to Deevee at Newmarket latest start: effective at 1m, and   112 Nm   8f
stays 1¼m: acts on firm and dead going: sometimes sweating: front runner. *M.
BELL*
    7-11   Drawn 17                 D. Harrison (3)
    *Red, grey sash, grey and red striped sleeves, quartered cap (Mr A. M. Warrender)*

**17 FAIRY STORY (IRE)** 3 ch.f. Persian Bold 123 – Certain Story (Known Fact **111**
1906    (USA) 135) [1992 5.7f⁴ 5m³ 6g² 7g* 6.5m 7.6v⁵ :: 1993 7g² 7m* 7m* 7.1m Jul 2]   98 Ch   7m
angular filly: fairly useful handicapper: made all at Epsom and Chester in June,   91 Ep   7m
going clear from 2f out to beat Diwali Dancer by 5 lengths on second occasion:   77'Ba   6f
favourite, ran poorly in £7,400 event at Sandown latest start: will stay 1m: suited
by a sound surface. *J. W. HILLS*
    7-10   Drawn 15                B. Doyle (3)
    *Royal blue and yellow diabolo, yellow sleeves, royal blue cap (The Fairy Story*
    *Partnership)*

**18 CEE-JAY-AY** 6 gr.g. Free State 125 – Raffinrula 75 (Raffingora 130) [1992 a8g³ **112**
2036    7.6g⁵ 8m a7g³ 8m⁶ 8.9d 7.5m³ 8g³ 7s* 7d⁵ 7.6v² 8.1d⁶ a8g :: 1993 a8g 8f* a8g³ 8d   104 Wa   7d
8g² 7.6f* 7v³ 8.1s² 8.1d³ 7d² 7m 7.6g⁵ Jul 9] smallish, workmanlike gelding:   103 Ha   8s
usually looks well: fair handicapper: won William Hill Spring Mile at Doncaster   101 Ch   8f
in March and £7,400 event at Chester in May: rare below-form effort at Chester
latest start: effective at 7f to 1m: acts on any going: below form when blinkered
once at 4 yrs: usually slowly away and is held up: effective for lady rider or
claimer: consistent. *J. BERRY*
    7-7 (7-4)   Drawn 18             L. Charnock
    *Emerald green, orange epaulets, orange cap (Mr Richard Jinks)*

**19 FIGHTER SQUADRON** 4 ch.g. Primo Dominie 121 – Formidable Dancer **108**
1771    70 (Formidable (USA) 125) [1992 a6g⁵ a5g 5s 5v² 5g a5g² a5g* a5g² 5.1g³ 5g² a6g⁴   98 Do   7g
a6g³ 5m* 6m³ 6m³ a5g 6m³ a6g⁶ a5g :: 1993 6m⁵ 6v 7g* 7g* 7g⁶ 7m Jun 26] leggy   97'Nm   6m
gelding: fair handicapper: won at Doncaster in tremendous style: had the   93 Nm   7g
ground against him next time and didn't do his best: runs latest start: effective at
6f to 7f: best form on sound surface and acts on foresand: usually visored or
blinkered nowadays: sometimes hangs markedly left. *J. A. GLOVER*
    7-7 (7-1)   Drawn 2            Darren Moffatt (5)
    *Light blue, pink epaulets, light blue sleeves, pink seams, quartered cap*
    *(Claremont Management Services)*

**20 QUEEN WARRIOR** 4 b.f. Daring March 116 – Princess Zenobia 72 (Record **108 p**
2125  Token 128) [1992 7d⁴ 8g* 7m² 8m² 8m a7g³ 8g 8d :: 1993 8.3d 8.3d* 8m* 8.3m*   109' Ke  8m
Jul 12] tall, leggy, sparely-made filly: successful in handicaps at Windsor (twice)   104' Yo  7m
and Carlisle (in between) this summer, quickening well from off pace to lead 2f   101 Wi  8m
out and beat Wakil 1½ lengths latest start: effective at 1m and will stay 1¼m: acts
on good to firm and dead ground: in fine form, and should continue to do well. *P. T. WALWYN*
   7-7 (6-11)  Drawn 14                               D. Wright (5)
   *Emerald green, black and emerald green striped sleeves, black cap (Mr Christopher Spence)*

STARTING PRICES: 5/1 Peter Davies, 13/2 Philidor, 8/1 Show Faith, 9/1 Abbey's Gal, Shamam, 10/1 Forever Diamonds, Blockade, 16/1 Stoney Valley, Lost Soldier, 20/1 Cumbrian Challenge, Northern Bird, Queen Warrior, 25/1 Pay Homage, 33/1 Double Flutter, Norfolk Hero, Fairy Story, Frogmarch, 40/1 Prenonamoss, 50/1 Cee-Jay-Ay

---

FOURTH RACE   (TV BBC2)               TRW  132  132  128  123  124  (Average 128)

---

## 4.15   THE KING GEORGE STAKES (A)          5f
## (Group 3)
### £30,000 added   3yo+   TWFA 3 9-12

---

**1 KEEN HUNTER (USA)** 6 ch.h. Diesis 133 – Love's Reward (Nonoalco **133**
2021  (USA) 131) [1992 5m⁶ 5s² 5s² 6g² :: 1993 6s² 6m⁴ Jul 8] tall, strong, good-topped   109 As  6s
horse: impresses in appearance: high-class performer: has had only 12 races,   101' Do  6g
including when winner and second in last 2 runnings of Prix de l'Abbaye at   101' Sa  5m
Longchamp: ran very well when length second to College Chapel in Cork And
Orrery Stakes at Royal Ascot: fair effort when 4 lengths fourth of 12 to Hamas in
July Cup at Newmarket 3 weeks later: effective at 5f and 6f: capable of very smart
form on good to firm, but needs give in the ground to show his best and acts on
soft going: bandaged near-hind this year: genuine. *J. H. M. GOSDEN*
   9-10  Drawn 7                               W. R. Swinburn
   *Maroon, white sleeves, maroon cap, white star (Sheikh Mohammed)*

**2 PARIS HOUSE** 4 gr.c. Petong 126 – Foudroyer (Artaius (USA) 129) [1992 5s* **128**
1549  5g² 5f 6g⁵ 5m 5m⁶ 5m :: 1993 5m* 5g* 5d³ Jun 18] strong, lengthy colt: improved   119 Sa  5g
form both when winning Palace House Stakes at Newmarket and UB Group   109' Yo  5m
Temple Stakes at Sandown in May: ran well when 2 lengths third of 8 to Elbio in   107 As  5d
King's Stand Stakes at Royal Ascot: best at 5f: acts on good to firm and soft
ground: visored (well beaten) final start at 3 yrs: tends to wander, but is genuine:
looked in tremendous condition at Ascot. *J. BERRY*
   9-8  Drawn 3                               J. Carroll
   *Maroon, beige sleeves, maroon armlets (Mr P. E. T. Chandler)*

**3 FREDDIE LLOYD (USA)** 4 ch.g. Barrera (USA) – Shredaline (USA) **123**
2021  (Shredder (USA)) [1992 5v³ 6g⁶ 5g* 5.1g² 5m* 5m* 5m* 5m⁵ :: 1993 5m 6d 5d⁴   122' Yo  5m
6m Jul 8] robust, good-quartered gelding: carries condition: has a roundish action:   103' Go  5m
vastly improved in 1992, gaining final win in King George Stakes at Goodwood:   96 As  5d
near best form (unimpressive in appearance previously) when fourth to Elbio in
King's Stand Stakes at Royal Ascot: 33/1, showed bright speed 5f then weakened
steadily in July Cup at Newmarket 3 weeks later: best at 5f: very best form on
top-of-the-ground, has run creditably on dead. *N. A. CALLAGHAN*
   9-5  Drawn 6                               J. Reid
   *Royal blue, white cross of lorraine and armlets, check cap (Mr Michael Hill)*

**4 ARTISTIC REEF** 4 ch.c. Claude Monet (USA) 121 – Kellys Reef 92 (Pitskelly **124**
2021  122) [1992 5.1g² 5g² 5.2g² 5m³ 5d* :: 1993 6g³ 5m⁴ 5m⁴ 5g⁶ 6m Jul 8] strong,   112' Nm  5m
workmanlike colt: unimpressive mover: useful performer: best effort when fourth   112' Nb  5g
in Palace House Stakes at Newmarket second start: fair sixth of 10 in Temple   107 Nm  5m
Stakes at Sandown, best effort since: 100/1, last of 12 in July Cup at Newmarket
last time: effective at 5f and 6f: acts on good to firm ground, simple task on dead:
sometimes hangs left. *G. H. EDEN*
   9-0  Drawn 2                               T. Quinn
   *Emerald green, white chevron, check cap (Mr R. A. Mohammed)*

5 **BLYTON LAD** 7 b.g. Skyliner 117 – Ballinacurra (King's Troop 118) [1992 5g³ **133 ?**
875 5m² 5f 5m² 5m 5m³ 5m* 5m² 6g* :: 1993 6d May 13] big, rangy gelding: impresses
in appearance: smart sprinter: successful last autumn in listed races at
Newmarket (Rous Stakes for third successive year) and Doncaster: pulled up
having burst a blood vessel in Duke of York Stakes in May: effective at 5f and 6f:
acts on firm and dead going: often sweating/edgy: used to be unruly in
preliminaries: has hung: tough and genuine. *M. J. CAMACHO*
    9-0  Drawn 1            S. Webster
*Red, white star, halved sleeves and star on cap (Mrs J. Addleshaw)*

    124' Nm 5m
    117' Do 6g
    111' Sa 5m

6 **EL YASAF (IRE)** 5 b.h. Sayf El Arab (USA) 127 – Winsong Melody (Music **125 ?**
2064 Maestro 119) [1992 5s⁵ 5g 5m⁵ 6g⁵ 5f⁵ 5g⁴ 5m 5m 6d 5m 5.2s 6s :: 1993 5.1m² 5g*
5d⁵ 5.1s⁴ Jul 10] small, sturdy horse: useful handicapper on his day: when sweating,
won listed rated stakes event at Epsom in June in very good style: for second
successive year appeared to excel himself by finishing fifth in King's Stand Stakes
at Royal Ascot: never able to land a blow in £9,700 minor event at Chester 3 weeks
later: best at 5f: probably acts on any ground. *T. J. NAUGHTON*
    9-0  Drawn 9            Pat Eddery
*Yellow and light blue diabolo, yellow cap (Mr J. Naughton)*

    120' As 5f
    104 Ep 5g
    100 As 5d

7 **BUNTY BOO** 4 b.f. Noalto 120 – Klairove 74 (Averof 123) [1992 6.1d* 6.1g **123**
2064 6m⁶ 5m⁶ 5.1g* 5m² 5s² 5s* 5m³ 6g :: 1993 5m⁶ 5d⁶ 5g 5d⁶ 5m² 5.1s³ Jul 10] leggy
filly: useful performer: ran well in pattern/listed company on first, fourth and fifth
outings, below best in handicaps in between: better than bare result suggests in
£9,700 minor event at Chester last time, weakening markedly final 1f behind
Stack Rock: best at 5f: acts on good to firm and soft ground: has worn crossed
noseband: successful for 7-lb claimer and when sweating: tough and game. *B. A.
MCMAHON*
    8-11  Drawn 10           A. Munro
*Yellow, royal blue stars, royal blue and yellow hooped sleeves, yellow cap, royal
blue star (Mrs R. C. Mayall)*

    113' Yo 5s
    109 Sa 5m
    106' Yo 5m

8 **GARAH** 4 b.f. Ajdal (USA) 130 – Abha 117 (Thatching 131) [1992 6m* 6.1g* **129**
1535 6m* 6m⁴ 5m² 5m⁵ 6g³ :: 1993 6g⁴ 6d² 5g³ 6s⁵ Jun 17] smallish, sturdy filly: good
walker: very useful performer: ran very well first 3 starts this year, placed in Duke
of York Stakes then Temple Stakes at Sandown: also performed better than bare
result suggests in Cork And Orrery Stakes at Royal Ascot, eventually winning
duel for lead over 2f out before fading into fifth of 19 behind College Chapel:
effective at 5f and stays 6f well: acts on good to firm and dead ground: has run
well when sweating and edgy *H. R. A. CECIL*
    8-11  Drawn 11          R. Cochrane
*Maroon, grey epaulets, grey cap, maroon star (Prince A. A. Faisal)*

    120 Sa 5g
    114' Nm 5m
    113 Nm 6g

9 **LOCHSONG** 5 b.m. Song 132 – Peckitts Well 96 (Lochnager 132) [1992 6v³ **135**
1936 6g* 6f⁴ 6m* 5.6m* 6d* 6d² :; 1993 5m³ 6d⁴ 5g⁴ 5g³ 5m* Jul 3] strong, lengthy
mare: impresses in appearance: improved no end in 1992 winning 3 major sprint
handicaps: contested pattern events next 5 starts, running well only when placed:
put up career-best performance latest start, making all to win 7-runner listed
event at Sandown by 4 lengths from Bunty Boo: effective at 5f to 6f: acts on any
going: has won for 7-lb claimer: races prominently: tough and genuine: looked
extremely well at Sandown and looks the ideal type for King George Stakes at
Goodwood. *I. A. BALDING*
    8-11  Drawn 5           L. Dettori
*Purple, light blue chevron, light blue cap (Mr J. C. Smith)*

    125 Sa 5m
    114' Do 6m
    113 Nm 5m

10 **MARINA PARK** 3 b.f. Local Suitor (USA) 128 – Mary Martin (Be My Guest **125**
2021 (USA) 126) [1992 5m² 5g* 5f⁴ 5d* 6g* 6s³ 6g² :: 1993 7g⁵ 6m⁵ Jul 8] quite
attractive filly: good mover: very useful form: respectable 3¾ lengths fifth of 8 to
Niche in Nell Gwyn Stakes at Newmarket on reappearance, taking keen hold:
12/1, very good 5½ lengths fifth of 12 to Hamas in July Cup at Newmarket nearly
3 months later: best at sprint distances: acts on any going. *M. JOHNSTON*
    8-11  Drawn 4          Dean McKeown
*Yellow, light green epaulets, light green and yellow striped cap (Greenland Park Ltd)*

    105' Nb 6g
    102' As 6g
    101' Sa 5d

11 **SOVEREIGN GRACE (IRE)** 4 gr.f. Standaan (FR) 118 – Gay Nocturne 63 **118**
(Lord Gayle (USA) 124) [1992 7g⁴ 5g* 5m :: 1993 5s 5g² Jul 1] small, lengthy Irish
filly: has raced only 5 times so far: won maiden at Tipperary last August and not
disgraced in listed event at Doncaster 3 weeks later: 16/1, showed vastly
improved form when short-head second of 8 to Rosie's Mac in listed event at
Tipperary after 6-week break last time, headed near line: very speedy: easily best
effort on good ground. *J. G. BURNS, IRELAND*
    8-11  Drawn 8          J. Murtagh
*Maroon, white spots, white cap, maroon spots (Lady Clague)*

STARTING PRICES: 13/8 Lochsong, 4/1 Keen Hunter, 9/2 Paris House, 9/1 Marina Park, 10/1 Garah, 16/1
Blyton Lad, 20/1 El Yasaf, 25/1 Freddie Lloyd, 33/1 Bunty Boo, 50/1 Artistic Reef, Sovereign Grace

# 4.45 THE KINRARA STAKES (HANDICAP) (C)
## 7f

£7,000 added  3yo  (Rated 0-90)

---

**1** **EMBANKMENT (IRE)** 3 b.c. Tate Gallery (USA) 117 – Great Leighs 87 **98**
1550 (Vaigly Great 127) [1992 6g$^6$ 6m$^3$ 6s$^2$ 7m$^4$ 7.3g$^2$ 7.9d$^4$ 7s$^3$ 7m$^3$ :: 1993 8m* 7g$^6$
8.1d$^3$ 7.9d$^4$ 7g$^2$ 8d Jun 18] good-quartered colt: fairly useful handicapper: won
maiden at Leicester in March: first disappointing effort this year at Royal Ascot
latest start: effective at 7f to 1m: acts on good to firm ground and dead, below form
on soft: consistent. *R. HANNON*
9-7   Drawn 10                                    Mark Denaro (7)
*Rose pink, navy blue sleeves, gold cap (Lady Tennant)*

| | |
|---|---|
| 91 Yo | 8d |
| 90 Sa | 8d |
| 90 Nm | 7g |

**2** **WISHAM (USA)** 3 ch.c. Be My Guest (USA) 126 – Massorah (FR) 108 **99**
2253 (Habitat 134) [1992 6g$^5$ 7g$^3$ :: 1993 7g 7.1s$^3$ 7.1s$^3$ 7g$^2$ 7.1g$^2$ 7g* 8d$^5$ Jul 17] tall,
good-topped colt: has plenty of scope: fairly useful: won maiden at Lingfield
in July by 3 lengths: best effort: colt: faded when to Beauchamp Hero in rated
stakes handicap at Newmarket week later: may well be ideally suited by 7f: acts
on soft going, yet to race on top of the ground: bandaged last 3 starts: takes strong
hold. *B. HANBURY*
9-1   Drawn 13                                       M. Hills
*Emerald green and royal blue (halved horizontally), blue sleeves, quartered cap
(Mr P. G. Goulandris)*

| | |
|---|---|
| 93 Ha | 7g |
| 82 Sa | 7s |
| 79'Do | 7g |

**3** **SIMPLY FINESSE** 3 b.g. Simply Great (FR) 122 – Spring In Rome (USA) **100**
2157 (Forli (ARG)) [1992 6m$^4$ 5m$^4$ 5g$^3$ 6m$^2$ 6g 7g$^4$ :: 1993 8g$^2$ 7g* 7g 6m$^6$ 7.1s$^2$ Jul 14]
leggy, angular gelding: fairly useful performer: won maiden at Goodwood in May:
usually held up, but always front rank when very good second of 15 to Fourforfun
in handicap at Sandown latest start: effective at 7f to 1m: yet to race on firm going,
acts on any other. *R. AKEHURST*
8-11   Drawn 8                                       T. Quinn
*Brown and white (quartered), brown sleeves, white cap (Food Brokers Ltd)*

| | |
|---|---|
| 100 Go | 7g |
| 92'Go | 6m |
| 88 Sa | 7s |

**4** **ARID** 3 b.c. Green Desert (USA) 127 – Fabulous Luba (Luthier 126) [1992 NR :: **100**
2209 1993 8d$^5$ 8g 7g$^3$ 7g* 8m 7g* Jul 16] good-bodied colt: half-brother to 7f and 1m
winner Kristal Rock (by Kris) and 2 winners abroad, including multiple Italian
middle-distance winner Luba Ley (by Shirley Heights): dam, second twice over
1m in France, is daughter of Altesse Royale: made all in maiden at Redcar in June
and always prominent in steadily-run race to win 12-runner handicap (by short
head from Teanarco) at Newbury in July: stays 1m: acts on good to firm and dead
going: visored (ran poorly) penultimate start: sometimes gives trouble in
preliminaries: has had tongue tied down. *J. H. M. GOSDEN*
8-13   Drawn 12                                      L. Dettori
*Maroon, white sleeves, maroon cap, white star (Sheikh Mohammed)*

| | |
|---|---|
| 93 Go | 7g |
| 57 Nb | 7g |
| 53 Nb | 8d |

**5** **CHILI HEIGHTS** 3 br.c. Chilibang 120 – Highest Tender 56 (Prince **99**
2157 Tenderfoot (USA) 126) [1992 5g$^5$ 5d$^4$ 5.7g$^4$ 6g$^6$ 6m$^3$ 6d$^6$ 6s* 7g$^4$ :: 1993 6g 6g 6m$^3$
6d 7.1s$^3$ Jul 14] compact colt: fairly useful handicapper: close third at Salisbury in
June: well beaten since in Wokingham at Royal Ascot then fair never-nearer third
of 15 to Fourforfun at Sandown: stays 7f: acts on good to firm and soft going:
bandaged behind last 2 starts. *G. B. BALDING*
8-12   Drawn 9                                       J. Williams
*Black, gold spots on body and cap (Mr B. T. Attenborough)*

| | |
|---|---|
| 99'Do | 7g |
| 97'Nb | 6s |
| 86'Sb | 5d |

**6** **KNIGHT OF SHALOT (IRE)** 3 b.g. Don't Forget Me 127 – Lady of Shalott **98**
2178 61 (Kings Lake (USA) 133) [1992 6d :: 1993 7m$^2$ 7g* 8.5m$^3$ 7d Jul 15] strong,
lengthy gelding: 7/4 on, easy winner of maiden at Thirsk in June: creditable third
in handicap at Beverley next start: well-backed favourite though facing fairly stiff
task, below form in similar event at Catterick 12 days later: stays 8.5f: acts on good
to firm going. *P. W. CHAPPLE-HYAM*
8-11   Drawn 3                                  Stephen Davies (5)
*Emerald green, royal blue sleeves, white cap, emerald green spots (Mr R. E.
Sangster)*

| | |
|---|---|
| 90 Bv | 8m |
| 87 Ep | 7m |
| 74 Th | 7g |

**7 FIELD OF VISION (IRE)** 3 b.g. Vision (USA) – Bold Meadows 80 (Persian **98**
2129 Bold 123) [1992 5g⁴ 5s⁵ 5.1s 5m⁶ 5m² 5m* 5g 5f⁵ 5g⁴ 5g³ :: 1993 7m* 7.1g⁴ 7g² 7m* — 85 Sa 7m
7.1m* 7m 7.5f² Jul 13] neat, quite attractive gelding: has a quick action: has — 83'Hm 5m
progressed into a fairly useful handicapper: won at Lingfield in May, Redcar in — 73'Re 5g
June and Sandown (quickened well) in July: good 6-length second of 5 to Tahdid
at Beverley last time, staying on well: stays 7.5f well: acts on firm ground, has not
raced on a soft surface since very early in career: seemed best in blinkers at 2 yrs,
but has done nothing wrong without them this season. *M. JOHNSTON*
8-11 Drawn 4 T. Williams
*Emerald green, red stripe, halved sleeves, emerald green and red striped cap (Mr*
*R. W. Huggins)*

**8 AL MOULOUKI** 3 b.g. Efisio 120 – Prejudice 83 (Young Generation 129) **94**
2294 [1992 6g 7d 6s⁵ 7d :: 1993 6.9s⁶ 7s 6g 7.1m* 8.1d* 7s* 7m* 8.2v⁵ 6m 6g⁵ Jul 19] — 81 Ed 8d
good-topped gelding: has a round action: progressed into a fair handicapper this — 76 Le 7m
spring, winning at Edinburgh (twice), Catterick and Leicester: given a break after — 76 Ct 7s
next start, and campaigned over inadequate trip, not at all disgraced, since return:
needs further than 6f, and stays 1m: acts on soft and good to firm going: shouldn't
be written off. *J. W. PAYNE*
8-10 Drawn 15 R. Cochrane
*Light green, royal blue stars, light green sleeves, light green cap, royal blue star*
*(Mr G. Jabre)*

**9 SECOND CHANCE (IRE)** 3 ch.c. Digamist (USA) 110 – Flash Donna (USA) **100**
2157 70 (Well Decorated (USA)) [1992 5g⁴ 5d 5g 5m³ 5d 5g* 5g⁴ 5g⁴ 6d² 5g 5.2g⁵ 5.1d² — 87 Br 6g
6s³ 5g³ :: 1993 6s² 6g² 5d⁶ 7m 6g⁴ 7d² 7m 7.6g* 7.1s Jul 14] sparely-made — 86 Ya 6g
colt: poor mover: fair handicapper: won minor event at Lingfield in July: well — 86'Nb 6s
below form on soft ground at Sandown 5 days later: stays 7f: acts on good to firm
ground and dead: wore a visor (which slipped) fifth start at 2 yrs: ridden with
forcing tactics last 3 starts. *P. MITCHELL*
8-8 Drawn 6 W. Newnes
*White, red cross of lorraine, emerald green sleeves, white armlets, red and white*
*hooped cap (Down and Outs Racing)*

**10 THE LITTLE FERRET** 3 ch.c. Scottish Reel 123 – Third Movement 75 **99**
2336 (Music Boy 124) [1992 6s² :: 1993 6g² 8d 7m⁴ 6.9m 7g² 8m³ Jul 22] leggy colt: fair — 102'Nb 6s
maiden: returned to form when second at Lingfield penultimate start, always — 98 Li 7g
prominent and running on well: tried to match strides with impressive winner El — 83 Fo 6g
Duco at Brighton 12 days later, quickly brushed aside final 2f but no discredited:
probably stays 1m: acts on soft ground, probably on good to firm. *R. HANNON*
8-8 Drawn 14 B. Rouse
*Royal blue, white cross of lorraine, red cap, white spots (Mr K. Higson)*

**11 HUNTERS OF BRORA (IRE)** 3 b.f. Sharpo 132 – Nihad 76 (Alleged (USA) **98+**
2055 138) [1992 NR :: 1993 8g⁶ 7d* 7.9m⁶ Jul 9] sturdy, lengthy filly: third foal: — 84 Yo 8m
half-sister to middle-distance maiden Shining Wood (by Touching Wood): dam — 50 Ay 7d
maiden suited by 1¼m, is out of half-sister to very smart sprinter/miler Clever — 50 Ca 8g
Trick: narrowly won slowly-run maiden at Ayr in June: faced extremely stiff task
in £7,000 minor event at York 3 weeks later and not at all discredited though
around 10 lengths sixth of 7 to Thourios, hanging right: stays 1m: acts on good to
firm and dead ground: likely to improve again. *J. D. BETHELL*
8-6 Drawn 5 A. Munro
*Royal blue, white spots and sleeves, scarlet cap (Mr Robert Gibbons)*

**12 BELFRY GREEN (IRE)** 3 ro.c. Doulab (USA) 115 – Checkers (Habat 127) **98**
1189 [1992 NR :: 1993 8d 8g 7g² 8.1s⁶ May 31] lengthy colt: unimpressive mover: fifth — 103 Go 7g
foal: brother to 1m winner Mitsubishi Video and half-brother to Irish 1m winner — 69 Cp 8s
Larnaca (by Shernazar): dam placed on Irish 1m and half-sister to dam of
Sarcita from family of Sarah Cranberry Sauce: easily best effort in maidens when
second to Simply Finest at Goodwood in May: looked less than keen latest start:
should stay beyond 7f: takes good hold and wears crossed noseband. *C. A.*
*HORGAN*
8-3 Drawn 1
*Emerald green, yellow epaulets, halved sleeves, yellow cap (Mr John Kelsey-Fry)*

**13 HALLORINA** 3 b.f. Hallgate 127 – Diorina 91 (Manacle 123) [1992 5g 6f⁵ 5.1f **97**
2126 6m* 6.1g* 6m* 6g 6.5m 5.2g :: 1993 5.7m* 5.1m* 6d³ 6m 6m Jul 12] smallish filly: — 103'Go 6m
unimpressive mover: fair handicapper: improved form when winning twice at — 91 Wi 6d
Bath in May: below her best since: effective at 5f and 6f: best form on good to firm — 86 Ba 6m
going. *W. G. R. WIGHTMAN*
7-11 Drawn 7 G. Bardwell
*Red, black cross belts and cuffs, lavender sleeves (Mrs J. A. Thomson)*

**14  WALNUT BURL (IRE)**  3 b.c. Taufan (USA) 119 – Hay Knot (Main Reef 126)  **98**

2144  [1992 5m⁴ 6m 6d³ 6m⁵ 6s⁴ 6s :: 1993 6s 6g³ 7m* 7m 7.1g 7d⁶ 7.1m 7g⁶ Jul 13]    91 Li    7m
rather leggy, quite attractive colt: easily best effort (rated 67) when promoted    88'Le    5m
winner of maiden at Lingfield in May: has run poorly last 3 starts: better at 7f than    84'Go    6s
shorter and is worth a try at 1m: acts on good to firm and soft ground: one to treat
with caution. *L. J. HOLT*
   7-7  Drawn 2                                                           N. Adams
   *Red, yellow sash, blue cap (Mr G. Steinberg)*

**15  DESERT NOMAD**  3 b.f. Green Desert (USA) 127 – Pale Gold (FR) (New  **99**

2118  Chapter 106) [1992 6g 5d⁶ 6s :: 1993 6g a7g³ 10g 7m⁴ 7m* 7f* 7m⁶ Jul 12]    102 Br    7f
good-topped filly: unimpressive mover: fair performer: won maiden handicap    83'Li    5d
and minor event (by short head) at Brighton this summer: below form in handicap    73 Br    7m
at Southwell 11 days later: stays 7f (pulled up over 1¼m as saddle slipped): acts
on firm and dead going. *S. DOW*
   7-7  Drawn 11                                                          D. Wright (5)
   *White, orange cross belts (Eurostrait Ltd)*

STARTING PRICES: 100/30 Simply Finesse, 6/1 Arid, 7/1 Hunters of Brora, 9/1 Al Moulouki, Field of Vision,
10/1 Chili Heights, 12/1 Embankment, 14/1 Knight of Shalot, The Little Ferret, 16/1 Second Chance, Desert
Nomad, 20/1 Hallorina, 25/1 Walnut Burl

---

SIXTH RACE

## 5.20  THE LAVANT NURSERY STAKES (HCAP) (C)  6f

### £7,000 added   2yo

---

**1  BEST KEPT SECRET**  2 b.c. (Mar 11) Petong 126 – Glenfield Portion 86  **90 p**

1527  (Mummy's Pet 125) [1992 5f⁵ 5d* 5.1m² 5s* 6g² Jun 16] neat colt: has a quick    82 Ri    6g
action: sixth live foal: brother to winning sprinter Bernstein Bette and half-    77 Nc    5s
brother to winning sprinter Glenfield Greta (by Gabitat): dam 2-y-o 5f winner well    75 Th    5d
beaten at 3 yrs: successful in seller (bought in 6,000 gns) at Doncaster and minor
events at Thirsk and Newcastle: good second in minor events at Chester and
Ripon (beaten a length by Zuno Star) otherwise: stays 6f: acts on any going:
progressive. *J. BERRY*
   9-7  Drawn 2                                                          J. Carroll
   *Black, yellow cross of lorraine, striped sleeves, yellow cap (Manny Bernstein*
   *(Racing) Ltd)*

**2  JACOB BOGDANI**  2 ch.c. (Mar 21) Night Shift (USA) – Green's Collection 65  **83 p**

1990  (High Top 131) [1993 5.1m² 6.1m² 5.7f* Jul 7] workmanlike colt: good mover: first    79 Ba    6f
foal: dam stayer: ru~~nner-up in maiden before winning similar~~ event at Bath    61 Ba    5m
comfortably by 3½ len~~gths from Ashkernazy showing im~~proved form: will be at    60 No    6m
least as effective at 7f: yet to race on an easy surface: on the upgrade. *P. F. I. COLE*
   9-3  Drawn 8                                                          T. G. McLaughlin (7)
   *White, red cap, white spots (Richard Green (Fine Paintings))*

*[handwritten: non-runner]*

**3  MACIZO**  2 b.c. (Apr 24) Aragon 118 – Free On Board 73 (Free State 125) [1993  **78**

2122  6g⁶ 6.1m⁵ 5m³ Jul 12] strong, close-coupled colt: fourth foal: closely related to a    76 Wi    5m
winner in Hong Kong and half-brother to 3-y-o Remember The Night (by Petong):    57 No    6m
dam stayed 1¼m: progressive colt: over 2 lengths third of 11 to Cragganmore in    49 Wi    6g
median auction maiden at Windsor: stays 6f. *L. J. HOLT*
   9-1  Drawn 9                                                          A. Munro
   *Red, yellow sash, blue cap (Mr G. Steinberg)*

**4  VERCINGETORIX (IRE)**  2 br.c. (Mar 20) Gallic League 119 – Noble Nancy  **92 p**

2039  (Royal And Regal (USA)) [1993 5.2g 6.1m 5.1g* Jul 9] 10,500F, 15,500Y: tall colt:    77 Ch    5g
has scope: easy mover: seventh foal: half-brother to 1m seller winner Dusky
Nancy and a winner in Norway (both by Red Sunset): dam Irish 1¾m winner: still
not fully wound up, much improved form when making all in 7-runner maiden at
Chester, hanging right into straight but beating Yawara by a neck, pair clear: will
stay 6f: will do better. *G. LEWIS*
   8-10  Drawn 1                                                         Paul Eddery
   *Straw, brown check cap (Lord Hartington)*

**5 MILLICENT NORTH** 2 b.f. (Jan 12) Northern State (USA) 91 – Pattis Pet **80**

2203 (Mummy's Pet 125) [1993 6.1g³ 6g⁴ 6g Jul 16] 2,500Y: strong, lengthy filly: fourth foal: half-sister to 1990 2-y-o 7f winner Black Armorial (by Petong): dam lightly-raced daughter of stayer Blickling: stayed on when in frame in median auction maidens won by Second Sight at Chepstow and Bluegrass Prince at Windsor: below form in Newbury maiden latest start: will be better suited by 7f: tended to hang first 2 starts. *P. G. MURPHY*

| | | |
|---|---|---|
| 70 Wi | 6g | |
| 67 Cp | 6g | |

8-9 Drawn 3        J. Williams

*Emerald green, yellow cross of lorraine, sleeves and spots on cap (Mr K. F. Hogan)*

**6 CONNECT (IRE)** 2 b.g. (May 4) Waajib 121 – My My Marie (Artaius (USA) **87**

1246 129) [1993 5g 5.2g⁵ 6f* 6g⁶ Jun 2] 13,000F: useful-looking gelding: has a round action: half-brother to 3-y-o 1¼m winner Don't Forget Marie (by Don't Forget Me) and 2 winners abroad: dam lightly-raced daughter of sister to Cheveley Park winner Pasty: made all, quickening modest pace from over 1f out, when winning 6-runner maiden auction at Brighton by 5 lengths: readily outpaced from halfway in listed race at Epsom 6 days later: stays 6f. *B. J. MEEHAN*

| | | |
|---|---|---|
| 71 Br | 6f | |
| 67 Nb | 5g | |
| 65 Ep | 6g | |

8-9 Drawn 4        B. Rouse

*Light blue, dark blue cross belts and armlets, dark blue and light blue hooped cap (Mrs J. A. Hannon)*

**7 SWEET WHISPER** 2 gr.f. (Mar 29) Petong 126 – Softly Spoken 87 (Mummy's **79+**

2442 Pet 125) [1993 5f⁶ 5.3g* 5d³ 6g⁴ 5.3f² 6.1d 6m³ Jul 26] 12,500Y: leggy filly: has a quick action: first foal: dam sprinter: ~~non-runner~~ maiden at Brighton in April: better for ~~the~~ first ~~run since~~ stays ~~6f~~: acts on firm and dead ground: effective with or without blinkers. *R. HANNON*

| | | |
|---|---|---|
| 72 Wi | 5d | |
| 59. Br | 5g | |
| 59 Do | 5f | |

8-8 Drawn 12        M. Hills

*Maroon, light blue sleeves, light blue cap, maroon diamond (Mr P. D. Savill)*

**8 KNIGHTRIDER** 2 b.c. (Mar 28) Full Extent (USA) 113 – New Street (USA) 53 **84**

1993 (Our Native (USA)) [1993 5m⁴ 6g 5.1d⁴ 6m Jul 7] neat colt: first foal: dam 2-y-o 6f winner: plating-class maiden: little show from poor draw at Kempton latest start: should stay 6f: best run on dead ground, fair effort on good to firm. *C. JAMES*

| | | |
|---|---|---|
| 85 No | 5d | |
| 65 Li | 5m | |

8-5 Drawn 11        T. Quinn

*Black, yellow epaulets, striped sleeves and star on cap (Mr Paul De Weck)*

**9 SPORTING HEIR (IRE)** 2 b.c. (May 10) Anita's Prince 126 – Royal Accord **84**

2418 (King of Spain 121) [1993 5g 5m⁶ 5.1d⁶ 5g² a6g* Jul 24] IR 3,200Y: leggy colt: shows knee action: first foal: dam Irish 2m winner: much improved since being blinkered, making all, ~~ridden~~ by 4 lengths from Window Display, in seller at Southwell (retained 5,600 gns): stays 6f: acts on fibresand: free to post first 2 starts. *M. D. I. USHER*

| | | |
|---|---|---|
| 80 Li | 5g | |
| 49 Le | 5m | |
| 45 Ba | 5d | |

8-4 Drawn 5 (blinkers)        N. Adams

*Yellow, black diamond, black and yellow halved sleeves, yellow cap, black diamond (Sporting Partners)*

**10 CHIEF EXECUTIVE** 2 b.c. (Jan 19) Unfuwain (USA) 131 – Two Worlds **88**

2174 (USA) 68 (Diesis 133) [1993 6m 6g⁴ 7m 7d³ Jul 15] strong colt: thriving physically: active type: first foal: dam lightly raced stayed 7f: plating-class form: didn't appear to handle track all that well but still only third to Extra Bonus when apparently very favourably handicapped in nursery at Catterick: will stay 1m: form only on an easy surface. *N. A. CALLAGHAN*

| | | |
|---|---|---|
| 85 Ct | 7d | |
| 84 Nm | 6g | |

7-12 Drawn 7        D. Harrison (3)

*Emerald green, white cap, red star (Mr Yahya Nasib)*

**11 GINGERILLO** 2 ch.c. (Feb 1) Aragon 118 – Titian Beauty (Auction Ring (USA) **83**

1993 123) [1993 5m³ 6g 6m Jul 7] compact colt: second foal: half-brother to 3-y-o Petite Lass (by Lidhame), 5f winner at 2 yrs: dam poor daughter of sister to top-class sprinter Deep Diver and half-sister to Irish 2000 Guineas winner King's Company: showed plating-class form on debut but soundly beaten in similar company since: refused to enter stalls and withdrawn from nursery at Folkestone (blinkered) latest intended start. *T. G. MILLS*

| | |
|---|---|
| 72 Le | 5m |

7-9 Drawn 6 (blinkers)        D. Wright (5)

*Emerald green, pink chevron, diamonds on sleeves, emerald green cap, pink star (Mrs Val Morgan)*

**12 RISKIE THINGS** 2 ch.f. (Apr 18) Risk Me (FR) 127 – Foolish Things (Song **93**

2308 132) [1993 5f² 5s² 5.3g⁶ 5d 5m* 6g⁵ 6g² 5g³ Jul 20] 1,000Y: close-coupled filly: second foal: dam unraced: ridden by 7-lb claimer when winning 15-runner seller (bought in 6,800 gns) at Lingfield: creditable efforts in claimers next 2 starts, respectable third in Folkestone nursery latest outing: stays 6f: acts on any going: too free in visor third outing. *J. S. MOORE*

| | | |
|---|---|---|
| 91 Le | 6g | |
| 87 Ke | 5s | |
| 80 Do | 5f | |

7-7 Drawn 10

*White, maroon chevron, maroon and white striped sleeves and cap (Mr Terry Pasquale)*

---

STARTING PRICES: 7/2 Vercingetorix, Best Kept Secret, 6/1 Chief Executive, Connect, Millicent North, 8/1 Riskie Things, 11/1 Knightrider, 12/1 Macizo, 33/1 Gingerillo

# 5.50 THE DRAWING ROOM STAKES (HCAP) (D) 1m1f

£7,000 added   3yo+   (Rated 0-80)   TWFA 2 9-7

---

**1 HIGH LOW (USA)** 5 b.g. Clever Trick (USA) – En Tiempo (USA) (Bold Hour)  **86**
2199  [1992 8g* 7d² 8f⁴ 7g 8g 7m 8g 8m :: 1993 8g 8.3d³ Jul 16] sturdy, quite attractive
gelding: good mover: fairly useful performer: went really well first 3 starts (won
Lincoln) at 4 yrs: off course 2½ months, creditable third of 5 to Express Gift in
handicap at Hamilton last time, best of last 7 starts: effective at 7f to 1m: acts on
firm and dead ground: has gone well fresh: game front runner. *W. J. HAGGAS*
    10-0  Drawn 5                                                     S. Giles (7)
*White, red braces, black cap (Mr B. Haggas)*

| | |
|---|---|
| 96'As | 8f |
| 91'As | 7d |
| 87'Do | 8g |

**2 CAMDEN'S RANSOM (USA)** 6 b.g. Hostage (USA) – Camden Court  **89**
1905  (USA) (Inverness Drive (USA)) [1992 11.9m 10.8d 8m* 9g⁴ 8m* 8f⁶ 10d⁴ 8g⁵ 8m⁴
8.9m 10s⁶ 8.1g² 8d⁴ 9d 8g :: 1993 a10g³ a10g* 10.8f⁵ 9d² 10g* 10m² 10.1g 10s
10m⁶ Jul 2] good-bodied gelding: has a long stride: fairly useful handicapper: won
at Lingfield in March and Sandown (usually goes well there) in April: looking
very well, ran creditably in very valuable event at Sandown last time: suited by
strongly-run race at 1m to 1¼m: acts on good to firm and dead ground and on
equitrack (yet to race on fibresand): suitable mount for apprentice: held up. *D. R.
C. ELSWORTH*
    9-7  Drawn 6                                                     B. Doyle (3)
*Dark blue, white hoops, diabolo on sleeves (Mr Bob Cullen)*

| | |
|---|---|
| 91 Sa | 10g |
| 89 Wi | 10m |
| 83 Sa | 10m |

**3 ROYAL INTERVAL** 3 ch.g. Interrex (CAN) – Sister Rosarii (USA)  **81**
1925  (Properantes (USA)) [1992 5f⁶ 6m⁴ 7g³ 6s⁴ :: 1993 6m² 6.9g³ 6f 6m⁶ 8d² 8g* 8.5m*
Jul 3] strong, lengthy gelding: improved form when winning maiden at Brighton
in June and handicap at Beverley (by ½ length from Ribhi) in July: better at
around 1m than shorter: acts on good to firm ground and dead. *W. G. M. TURNER*
    9-7  Drawn 2                                                     D. McCabe (5)
*Red, light blue braces and sleeves, light blue and red quartered cap (Mr G. L.
Barker)*

| | |
|---|---|
| 73 Bv | 8m |
| 72 Br | 8g |
| 55 Ca | 8d |

**4 COURAGEOUS KNIGHT** 4 gr.g. Midyan (USA) 124 – Little Mercy 90 (No  **85**
2013  Mercy 126) [1992 6d 8.1m² 8.5d 7f* 8d⁵ 8m³ 8m⁶ :: 1993 8g 8.1s⁶ 10g⁴ 8s 10.2m³
10.2g³ Jul 8] lengthy gelding: fair handicapper: best efforts of season when third at
Chepstow on last 2 starts: stays 1¼m: best efforts on a sound surface and acts on
firm going. *R. HANNON*
    9-6  Drawn 7                                                     W. R. Swinburn
*White, royal blue epaulets, royal blue diamonds on sleeves and cap (Mr T. E.
Bucknall)*

| | |
|---|---|
| 74'Go | 8m |
| 72 Cp | 10g |
| 72'Cp | 8m |

**5 GOOGLY** 4 ch.f. Sunley Builds 102 – Cheri Berry 87 (Air Trooper 115) [1992 7d  **87**
2396  9.7g* 9g* 8m 9m³ 10g⁴ 10s² 10s* 12d² 9g² 11.9d* 12g² :: 1993 8d 8g 12g 10g² 10s²
10d² 8d⁵ Jul 24] leggy filly: unimpressive mover: fair handicapper: second at
Kempton, Sandown and Goodwood (beaten head by Bookcase) for 3 starts then
fair effort (ran well considering trip was too short) when fifth in £11,900 event at
Ascot last time: really needs further than 1m and stays 1½m: acts on good to firm
and soft ground: sometimes hangs and carries head awkwardly: tough. *W. G. R.
WIGHTMAN*
    9-6  Drawn 12                                                    J. Reid
*Grey, pink sleeves (Mr A. G. Lansley)*

| | |
|---|---|
| 88 Sa | 10s |
| 84 Ke | 10g |
| 83'As | 12g |

**6 HADEER'S DANCE** 3 b.c. Hadeer 118 – Harvest Dance 79 (Mill Reef (USA)  **83**
2295  141) [1992 6m⁴ 6f⁵ 7m* 7.5d⁶ 8.1d :: 1993 8g³ 7g⁴ 8d 8.3g⁵ Jul 19] good-topped
colt: unimpressive mover: best effort in Leicester handicap on reappearance: well
beaten in Britannia Handicap at Royal Ascot and steadily-run minor event at
Windsor on last 2 starts: better at 1m than shorter: easily best form on an easy
surface, though has won on good to firm. *R. W. ARMSTRONG*
    9-2  Drawn 4                                                     L. Piggott
*Pink, emerald green epaulets and armlets, emerald green and pink hooped cap
(Mr Khalifa Dasmal)*

| | |
|---|---|
| 71'Do | 7m |
| 55 Le | 8g |
| 52 Li | 7g |

**7 NORTH ESK (USA)** 4 ch.g. Apalachee (USA) 137 – Six Dozen (USA) (What  **84**
2250  A Pleasure (USA)) [1992 8.5m 8f 8m 10g 10m³ 8m :: 1993 a6g⁵ a6g a8f a7g⁵ a10g⁶
a10g 9.7s 11.7s 8f² 8g* 8g² 8m* 8d 8d⁵ Jul 17] good-topped gelding: fair
handicapper: won at Goodwood and Salisbury in June: good fifth of 10 to Deevee
at Newmarket latest start: effective at 1m, and stays 1¼m: acts on good to firm
ground, dead and equitrack, seemingly not on very soft: often on edge. *D. A.
WILSON*
    9-2  Drawn 11                                                    A. Munro
*Yellow, purple hoops on body, check cap (Mr Alan J. Speyer)*

| | |
|---|---|
| 74 Go | 8g |
| 73 Br | 8g |
| 71'Po | 10m |

## 8 SCORCHED AIR

3 b.f. Elegant Air 119 – Misfire 56 (Gunner B 126) [1992 7s⁶ **80**

2295   6.9v³ :: 1993 8g³ 8.3m* 8.3g³ Jul 19] half-sister to Irish 7f (at 2 yrs) and 1¼m    64'Go   7s
winner Synergy (by Dominion): dam 1½m seller winner: fair form: won maiden   62 Br   8g
at Windsor in July: good third in minor event at Windsor 14 days later, dictating   56'Fo   7v
steady early pace: likely to stay beyond 1m: probably acts on any going. *J. W.
HILLS*

    9-0   Drawn 1                         M. Hills
    *Grey, yellow epaulets, grey sleeves, yellow seams, yellow cap (Mr Michael
    Wauchope)*

## 9 TICKERTY'S GIFT

3 b.c. Formidable (USA) 125 – Handy Dancer 87 (Green **79**

2413   God 128) [1992 6d 6g⁴ 7d⁵ :: 1993 9g⁶ 10m 10m⁴ Jul 24] good-topped colt: fair   66'Le   7d
form: creditable fourth, always prominent, to Preston Guild in handicap at   56'Nb   6g
Southwell in July: stays 1¼m. *R. HANNON*                 54 Go   9g

    8-12   Drawn 9   (blinkers)                  B. Rouse
    *Royal blue, white cross of lorraine, red cap, white spot (Mr K. Higson)*

## 10 LADY LACEY

6 b.m. Kampala 120 – Cecily (Prince Regent (FR) 129) [1992 9d **84**

2364   8d 8g* 8g³ 8.9g³ 7f 8.3g 8d³ 8g 10m³ 10s³ 10g² 9d⁴ 10.2s² 9s 10.2d³ 12.1s⁶ 10.3g⁴   82'Sb   10s
a10g⁴ a12g³ :: 1993 7s 8g² 9g 8d⁶ 10.2g 10.8d⁴ 9s* 8g³ Jul 23] rather lightly-made   81 As   8g
mare: moderate handicapper: won selling event (no bid) at Sandown in July by 12   77'Do   10g
lengths, leading over 1f out: well-backed favourite, neck third of 13 in apprentice
event at Ascot 9 days later, staying on well: effective from 1m to 1¼m: goes very
well on soft going: visored: usually set plenty to do: tough. *G. B. BALDING*

    8-4   Drawn 10   (visor)                   N. Varley (7)
    *Orange, emerald green star and star on cap (Mrs K. L. Perrin)*

## 11 GREEN'S CASSATT (USA)

5 ch.m. Apalachee (USA) 137 – Royally **82**

2426   Rewarded (USA) (Bold Forbes (USA)) [1992 a10g a7g 7.6g⁶ 8g 7g⁴ 8f* 8.2m* 8.3g³   87'No   8m
9.7m⁶ 8g³ 8g 10g :: 1993 12.3m⁵ 10m⁶ 10.3s² 10.8g⁶ Jul 24] leggy, angular mare:   82'Fo   10m
modest handicapper: ran creditably on reappearance and on third start this year:   82'Th   8f
sweating and on toes when below form on latest one: effective at 1¼m and 1½m:
acts on any going: held up: inconsistent. *W. M. BRISBOURNE*

    8-0   Drawn 3                          R. Lappin
    *Emerald green, red cross belts and armlets, quartered cap (Mr K. K. Baron)*

## 12 HOOCHIECOOCHIE MAN (IRE)

3 b.c. Taufan (USA) 119 – Regal **86**

1499   Entrance (Be My Guest (USA) 126) [1992 a8g⁴ :: 1993 a7g⁴ 8m 10.2s* 10.3g*   78 Ba   10s
11.4m 10d² Jun 14] tall, close-coupled colt: won maiden event at Bath in April   70 Wi   10d
and 19-runner minor event at Doncaster ~~late~~ in ~~May~~: good   70 Do   10g
second of 6 to War ~~length~~ clear ~~steadily-run~~ handicap at
Windsor last time: stays 1¼m: acts on soft ground, below best on good to firm:
sometimes flashes tail: should continue to run well in handicaps under suitable
conditions. *D. W. P. ARBUTHNOT*

    8-0   Drawn 8
    *Royal blue, yellow stripe, yellow sleeves, royal blue armlets and star on yellow
    cap (Mr Christopher Wright)*

## 13 GLISSO (IRE)

3 ch.c. Digamist (USA) 110 – Gulf Bird 71 (Gulf Pearl 117) **?**

723   [1992 6s⁵ 6d 6v :: 1993 6d May 3] strong, close-coupled colt: has a round action:   76'Go   6s
modest form (rated 54) on debut: joint favourite, always in rear in handicap at
Newcastle in May, finishing tailed off: trained until after then by L. Cumani: one
to be wary of. *M. C. PIPE*

    7-7 (7-6)   Drawn 13                  N. Adams
    *Dark blue, white sleeves, dark blue stars, dark blue cap, white star (Teknagro S.
    R. L.)*

STARTING PRICES: 3/1 Googly, 4/1 Lady Lacey, 8/1 Camden's Ransom, Hadeer's Dance, Scorched Air, 10/1 Royal Interval, 12/1 Courageous Knight, North Esk, 14/1 High Low, 16/1 Glisso, Tickerty's Gift, 33/1 Green's Cassatt

## 2.30 Lanson Champagne Vintage Stakes   7f

The first thing we notice is that the rating for the top horse, Prince Babar, is below the TRW figures but close enough to them to suggest he may scrape it if today's renewal is substandard. As it may well be. We shouldn't care to take short odds about him, though. Prince Babar has won one of his four races, and was a staying-on third in the July Stakes over six furlongs on his last appearance; he 'may well be even better suited by 7f', but, as with so many two-year-olds, his ability to act on the ground has to be taken on trust. The remainder are the usual bunch of lightly-raced types, without the 'feel' of quality about them one usually associates with a race of this description. Only Hannon of the leading trainers is represented, with Lomas, an Ela-Mana-Mou colt unbeaten in two starts: this one's commentary tells us he made heavy weather of a four-horse race at Sandown on his last appearance. Classic Sky and Mister Baileys look more promising horses than Lomas, and decidedly better prospects than Beautete, an unfashionably-bred maiden-race winner, and Mr Eubanks, trounced in a listed event on the second of two appearances. Classic Sky has won two out of four, and on his most recent start defeated Mister Baileys, who was having only his second outing and enjoyed no sort of run, into third place in a good-class race over this distance at Newbury. Not a race to get excited about. If there is a 'value' bet in it, it is Prince Babar each-way at 4/1, and most certainly not Mister Baileys at 13/8, for all that the latter did not have the run of the race at Newbury.

*Mister Baileys wins easily. In taking second place, Prince Babar runs as well as the TRW figures suggested he would. Classic Sky is beaten ten lengths.*

## 3.10 Tiffany Goodwood Cup   2m

This race was run over 21f until 1991, so, strictly speaking, the first three TRW figures could be construed as having no relevence. Nevertheless, Sonus still looks something of a 'good thing'. He was 'runner-up in the 1992 St Leger' over 14.6f; he 'should stay 2m'; he has shown the speed to be 'effective at 1½m' (most of his principal opponents here are back in distance after running at 2½m in the Ascot Gold Cup) and he 'acts on dead ground': what's more, he's bang in form, having 'returned to his best' when second, conceding weight, at Newmarket only two weeks previously. Assessor (second) did better in the Gold Cup than Arcadian Heights (a horse with a vicious streak, gelded after last season) and Daru. Assessor is a good stayer, but a mudlark who 'needs a truly-run race', and on what we know of the horses it is not to be anticipated, with no obvious pacemaker in the field, that he will have the speed under today's conditions to get the better of Sonus at this distance. At least, that's the way we see it, reading the Timeform Race Card. But not everyone gets a Timeform Race Card, and Assessor is favourite at 6/4 with Sonus at 4/1 (perhaps backers are put off by the fact the horse is visored for the first time) and 9/1 bar two. At those odds Sonus would be a cracking bet each-way were it not for the fact that he is a much better bet to win.

*Under a supremely confident ride from Eddery, Sonus runs out a 'cheeky' winner by a length. Assessor runs well in second.*

### 3.45 Schweppes Golden Mile (Handicap)    1m

The first handicap of the day, and, on the face of it, a highly competitive one with plenty of in-form horses. The betting takes a wide range. One is accustomed to seeing the ratings for these races concertinaed within 3 or 4 lb, so it is a matter of some surprise to see Philidor sticking out like a sore thumb, 3 lb clear. Philidor's form looks rock-solid, and is backed up by a timefigure of 120: on his last three appearances he was second in the Zetland Gold Cup, third (over today's distance) in the Royal Hunt Cup, and fourth (looking 'in magnificent shape') in the Royal Hong Kong Jockey Club Trophy: he is 'effective at 1m: probably acts on any going: has never been better'. Racegoers don't go to the expense of a Timeform Race Card to pass up bets like this one. And at 13/2 there is no reason why they should. The horse isn't even favourite!

*Philidor gets the call in a finish of short heads with the three-year-olds Lost Soldier and Show Faith.*

### 4.15 King George Stakes    5f

No problems with the distance on this occasion—this race has always been run over 5f. So we can say with confidence that on the evidence of the TRW figures Lochsong would have won each of the last five runnings. So, does that make her an odds-on chance to win this one? Hardly—seeing that the ratings for Keen Hunter and Blyton Lad are also above the TRW figures. Nevertheless, she is sure to start favourite. Keen Hunter is a very good sprinter, but he hasn't won since 1991, and the best of his most recent runs at 5f have been under conditions more testing than they are today; on the first of his two outings this year he was second over 6f on soft going at Royal Ascot. Blyton Lad's only run so far in 1993 saw him pulled up with a burst blood-vessel; he returns after an absence of two and a half months an unfancied 16/1 shot for a race in which he was second in 1992. Lochsong was a revelation in 1992 'winning 3 major sprint handicaps': on her latest start this season she 'put up career-best performance, making all to win 7-runner listed event at Sandown by 4 lengths': she is 'effective at 5f to 6f: acts on any going: tough and genuine: looks the ideal type for the King George Stakes at Goodwood'. Sure she does. But at 13/8 (.381) she is not the best value in the world, though she's value enough. Keen Hunter each-way at 4/1 (.200) in a race in which they bet 16/1 bar five has also to be considered. 11/8 on (.579) the pair is another possibility.

*Lochsong comes out of the mist just in front of Paris House and stays there to win by a head. Keen Hunter, who was slowly away, would have beaten the pair in another few strides.*

### 4.45 Kinrara Stakes (Handicap)   7f

No sensible backer wants to bet in every race and this is the sort of tightly-knit handicap some racegoers might be happy to pass up in favour of some refreshment. And they may be right. One's instinct, in a race like this, is to seek out a horse perhaps less exposed than its rivals; failing that, one likely to improve for being raced over the distance for the first time. The most lightly-raced member of the field is Hunters of Brora, a winner over 7f on dead ground from three starts and noted as 'likely to improve again': the only runner not to have essayed the distance is our old friend Hallorina, 'below her best' since winning at Bath and whose 'best form is on good to firm going'. So, not much joy with Hallorina, but Hunters of Brora has possibilities. The commentaries offer about as much encouragement as the ratings, the only note of any consequence being the tail-piece—'should not be written off'—on Al Moulouki, the bottom-rated. This gelding did well in the spring, winning handicaps at 7f and 1m: after a break he came back, for reasons we can only guess at, to run at an 'inadequate' 6f, not once but twice: well, he's back at an adequate distance now: he is one of only two horses in the race to have won on soft going, though several have shown form on it.

*Al Moulouki (9/1) comes from behind to take up the running inside the last furlong, going on to beat Field of Vision (9/1) and Hunters of Brora (7/1) by 1½ lengths and the same.*

## 5.20 Lavant Nursery Stakes (Handicap)    6f

Riskie Things is ridden by a 7 lb-claimer able to draw only 4 lb of his allowance, which effectively reduces her rating by 3 lb; with eight races behind her she is easily the most experienced member of the field, and therefore the least likely to improve significantly, one would imagine: her chance is not helped by her being drawn on the outside but one of the field. Of the others, only the top-weighted, Best Kept Secret, a 'progressive' colt trained by Jack Berry, has run more than four times. Which underlines how difficult these races can be at this time of year. Vercingetorix, effectively the top-rated now that Riskie Things carries overweight, was 'not fully wound up' when showing 'much improved form' to make all in a seven-runner maiden over 5f on good going at Chester on the last of three previous appearances: we know from the comment that this horse is out of a mare that won over 1¾m, so he should be well suited by this step up in distance: he is evidently just coming to himself, and is the only horse in the field to have won last time out; in addition he has the advantage of being drawn next to the stand rail, with Best Kept Secret one to his right. The fourth top, Chief Executive, has already had a run off a 'favourable' mark, when third in a nursery over 7f at Catterick; one would expect a two-year-old by Unfuwain out of a mare by Diesis to be better off going up in distance, not down. Allowance has to be made for the possibility that something will improve considerably racing on soft going for the first time, but with the draw in their favour this looks a case of Best Kept Secret and Vercingetorix against the field. Best Kept Secret has proven his ability on the ground, but from the points of view of chance at the weights and potential to improve further, Vercingetorix looks the better proposition. Vercingetorix 5/2 (.286) and Best Kept Secret 7/2 (.222) add up to just under even money. Remember, we are talking here of what we see as the 'true' odds, from which we will be able to judge whether the odds the bookmakers offer are attractive enough for a bet.

*Vercingetorix (7/2) comes into view inside the last furlong with the race won, and is well on top at the finish, winning by 1½ lengths from Millicent North, with Best Kept Secret (7/2) 3½ lengths away third.*

### 5.50 Drawing Room Stakes (Handicap)　1m1f

To end the day, another handicap. When the ground is soft, it pays strongly to favour those who have shown the ability to handle the conditions. Both Googly and Lady Lacey have won on soft ground in the period covered by the form figures, Googly at 1¼m and Lady Lacey at 9f. Googly hasn't won at less than 9f and 'stays 1½m', and Lady Lacey has won at 1m and is 'effective to 1¼m'. So Googly has the better chance on the ratings, but Lady Lacey, who 'goes very well on soft going', is perhaps the speedier and therefore likely to be better suited by the distance. Of the others, Camden's Ransom, High Low and North Esk are noted as acting on dead ground, Courageous Knight's 'best efforts are on a sound surface', and Hadeer's Dance has little form on a soft one. The evidence suggests that Googly (3/1) and Lady Lacey (4/1)—roughly 6/5—are the two most likely to win. Common sense dictates that in these circumstances it is better to go for the one at the longer odds, particularly when 4/1 Googly was available to those who moved early.

*Googly gets up on the line to beat Lady Lacey by a short head, Camden's Ransom finishing third.*

'Here's a nice soft cushion old boy—
Timeform says you don't like hard going.'

# Betting The Timeform Way:

## Synopsis

We have sought in 'Betting The Timeform Way' to tell some home truths about betting, not with the intention of putting the reader off but in the hope that he or she might join the small minority of punters that make a profit in the long run.

*'Put in popular language we can say that in the contest between the bookmaker and the haphazard backer it is a little less than 5/4 on the bookmaker in one race.'*

It simply isn't possible for the majority of backers to win in the long run, for the reason that punters are betting *against one another*. The bookmakers, acting as middle-men or brokers, have to make a living and those backers who show a profit do so only at the expense of the vast majority who lose.

The first step on the road to becoming a successful punter is to acquire a superior knowledge of the horses themselves. However, the work involved—digging out all the essential facts on thousands of horses in training—is well beyond the capacity of any one person. This is where the Timeform Organisation comes in. Timeform does all the hard groundwork necessary and provides the punter with the benefit of it through the weekly *Timeform Black Book*, the daily *Timeform Race Cards* and the *Timeform Perspective* form-book. A wealth of experience and thousands of hours of intensive study go into making Timeform's publications indispensable to the serious backer. The Timeform subscriber should see himself as a businessman who commissions a team of experienced and highly skilled specialists to keep him ahead of the game. More horses win races because their form said they had a good chance at the weights than for any other reason, and betting according to Timeform Ratings alone—concentrating on the Timeform two top-rated—yields around half of all the winners. But there are other considerations, the most important of them being the racing character of each horse—how its prospects are affected by such things as the distance of the race and the state of the going, etc. The Timeform Commentaries that appear for every runner on the *Timeform Race Cards* and for thousands of horses every week in the *Timeform Black Book* contain a wealth of such information.

*'Successful backing is all about the search for value. Of getting the best of the odds.'*

Timeform's founder Phil Bull once wrote that 'Those who bet for fun are unlikely to get their entertainment for nothing'. Betting for fun is a form of entertainment like any other, but long-term success demands a disciplined approach. The pursuit of VALUE is crucial. Put simply, the pursuit of 'value' is the pursuit of probable winners whose odds are longer than they should be. Horses are frequently beaten even when they are good value to bet on, so the importance of getting 'value' or 'over the odds' needs to be stressed. 'Bargain' is another word for 'value'. If you strike a bet at 5/1 on a horse whose true chance of winning—taking all considerations into account—is 3/1, then you've got a bargain. Never take 'under the odds'. It is an equally important discipline *not* to bet when the odds do not represent 'value', do not look a 'bargain'. The odds the bookmakers offer are, to a large degree, a matter of supply and demand and, taken together, they are weighted against the backer to provide the bookmaker with his potential profit margin. But the odds against an individual horse (or horses) in one race are not necessarily weighted against the backer. It is quite possible to find horses quoted at longer odds than they should be. Making a profit from betting is consistently a matter of discovering horses whose odds are greater than are commensurate with their real chance of winning, horses with a better chance of winning than is widely or generally supposed. 'Don't go with the crowd: wait until you're sure you know better than the crowd', as Phil Bull once put it.

*'The superiority of Tote dividends over starting prices is confined largely to winners above the 10/1 mark. Winners ridden by popular jockeys can be expected usually to pay less (or less well comparatively) on the Tote whatever their SPs.'*

Tote versus bookmakers. Which is better for the punter? Well, for the backer—especially the course backer—the bookmakers have one big advantage. You know what price you are getting about the horse. It is there on the bookmaker's board. You can go to town if the odds represent 'value', and if they don't you don't take them. Although projected dividends are displayed above the Tote windows, the actual Tote return isn't available until after the race, so if you bet on the Tote—even if you hold off until close to the 'off'—you cannot know for certain whether you are getting value or not. From the standpoint of the serious backer this is a very big argument indeed. There's one area where betting on the Tote is usually advantageous to the punter. Bookmakers aren't renowned for being enterprising where outsiders are concerned and such winners can pay much better dividends on the Tote.

*'The easy general answer to the question whether or not the ordinary stay-at-home punter should bet ante-post is NO; for the reason that ante-post prices are always weighted more heavily against the backer than subsequent starting prices.'*

The attraction of ante-post betting lies in the longer odds available. But the drawbacks to betting early to get the longer odds outweigh the advantages. A good deal of money that is bet ante-post is lost without a run. The possibility of a big price about a fancied contender in an important race may be forfeited by waiting, but highly competitive prices are usually available on the day as the major firms compete for business.

*'The problem when to bet win only and when to bet each-way is a complex one to which no definite answer can be given.'*

There are no hard and fast rules about each-way betting. Each bet must be considered on its merits. But, as a generalisation, most punters bet each-way in situations where it should usually be avoided, and vice-versa. The idea that it is more sensible to back a long-priced horse each-way than it is to back a short-priced one is mistaken. It may be reasonable, under certain circumstances, to accept ⅕ the odds that your horse will finish in the first *third* of a field of nine, but, in non handicaps, it is foolish to accept the same odds that it will finish in the first *tenth* of a field of thirty. Notwithstanding some differences with handicaps of 16 runners or more, the bigger the field the less sense, as a rule, is each-way betting. The other main point to remember is that the presence of short-priced horses in a race has the effect of making each-way betting—on all the runners—more favourable to the backer.

*'The person who goes into a betting shop to place his bets, or who phones them through to his bookmaker, is rather like the trainer who habitually sends out his runners carrying over-*

*weight. He or she may still win, but where's the sense in making things more difficult than they need be?'*

As we have said, the sensible advice to readers anxious to get the most from their betting is to go racing, where bets with bookmakers are tax free. For the off-course backer, faced with paying tax on his bets, the option of paying tax on his or her stake is more sensible than electing to have the tax deducted from the returns. But the tax should be incorporated into the intended stake and not paid on top of it. The difference this makes to the profit on any single bet is small, but it adds up and can make the difference between winning and losing in the long run. The effect of incorporating betting tax is to reduce the odds—6/4 becomes 5/4, 3/1 is 5/2, 5/1 is 9/2, 8/1 is 7/1, etc—and when the backer is thinking of betting at odds much shorter than 10/1 he or she must stop and consider whether the bet represents value at the effective odds.

*'It would be nice to think that the off-course backer has something going for him. And he has. The early-betting races.'*

In a minority of races—those on which prices are available from around 9.30 am—the off-course backer can snap up the value before the racegoer has a chance to get in on the act. 'Early-bird' prices are available on most racing days—usually for competitive handicaps—and this type of betting can be very rewarding provided you have done your homework.

*'There is no perfect staking system, and there can be no perfect staking system.'*

We hope the extensive section in this book dealing with staking systems succeeds in ramming home the message that no one can make up for an inability to back winners by manipulating stakes, by increasing or decreasing them after so many winners or losers. If a staking plan has some sound logical basis rooted in the nature of racing itself it may be worth consideration, but the idea that you can make a profit in the long run by taking advantage of sequences, or the 'law of averages', or by other mathematical jugglery, is nonsense. The size of your bet should be related to what you regard as the 'true chance' of the horse. True even-money chances may be expected to win once in two, whereas true 10/1 chances cannot be expected to win more than once in eleven. So you are entitled to have far more on a true even-money chance than you are on a true 10/1 chance.

*'A bold and adventurous punter, who is prepared to take a chance on a losing run coming at the beginning, will operate from a much smaller bank than would a cautious man or woman, who prefers to allow for the worst to happen right at the start. It is all a question of temperament.'*

Our advice on fixing the size of your betting bank is to be cautious, and to bet within your means. Your bank should be big enough to provide *reasonable* protection against the inevitable losing periods. Always remember—especially when betting on credit—that you're betting in money, real money, and never chase your losses. Trying to get back in a single bet what you've lost—for example on the last race of the day, the traditional 'getting out' stakes—is a recipe for disaster. Likewise, don't fritter away your winnings by increasing your stakes because it's 'the bookies' money'. It isn't. When you've won it, it's yours.

In conclusion, always remember the importance of self control. Remember at all times that you are seeking one thing only: VALUE. Bet only when you think you're getting a bargain, when you're getting over the odds. Successful betting hinges on recognising probable winners whose odds are longer than they should be. If all your bets are sound ones, you'll win in the long run.

B.A.